Karl Decker, Angus McSween

Historic Arlington

Vol. 2

Karl Decker, Angus McSween

Historic Arlington
Vol. 2

ISBN/EAN: 9783337407223

Printed in Europe, USA, Canada, Australia, Japan

Cover: Foto ©ninafisch / pixelio.de

More available books at **www.hansebooks.com**

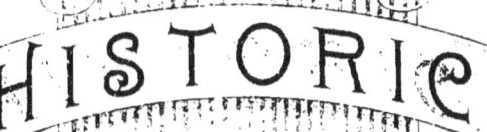

Historic Arlington.

A HISTORY OF THE NATIONAL CEMETERY FROM ITS ESTABLISHMENT TO THE PRESENT TIME, WITH SKETCHES OF THE HISTORIC PERSONAGES WHO OCCUPIED THE ESTATE PREVIOUS TO ITS SEIZURE BY THE NATIONAL GOVERNMENT—PARKE CUSTIS AND HIS TIMES—THE CAREER OF LEE, WITH DESCRIPTIONS OF LIFE IN VIRGINIA DURING THE EARLY PART OF THE CENTURY.

By KARL DECKER and ANGUS McSWEEN.

Published by the Decker and McSween Publishing Company,
Washington, D. C.

Entered according to act of Congress, in the year 1892, by
KARL DECKER and ANGUS McSWEEN,
in the Office of the Librarian of Congress, at Washington.

PREFACE.

In presenting this work to the public the authors feel that notwithstanding the labor and care exercised in its preparation the subject is one which is capable of still greater development. A complete history of the famous old place would be a history of the development of American political institutions and customs, the history of modes and fashions now long extinct, and the intellectual, moral, and industrial changes that have taken place in the land from the time the colonists first severed with their swords the knot that bound them to Great Britain, and set up a people's government under the protecting folds of the stars and stripes. For with all this is Arlington closely associated.

In the present volume the authors have endeavored to show the historic importance of the place, and in doing so present for the first time an authentic account of Parke Custis and the state of society during his lifetime, together with such portions of the history of General Lee as are connected with the estate. The occupation of Arlington by the Federal troops, its seizure by the United States, the legal proceedings by which the Government perfected its title, the establishment of the national cemetery and its growth to the present time, are all described in the work with a completeness of detail such as the subject demands.

The fact that so little was known, or could be learned, by the general public concerning Arlington caused the authors to undertake the publication of this volume, and they feel assured that its value to every student of American history, as well as to the many whose comrades and relatives lie beneath the Arlington sod, will be recognized and appreciated. In preparing the work the authors obtained their information from the records of the War Department, the personal recollections of men now living who were connected with some of the different phases of Arlington history, and from the collection of historic documents in the possession of Dr. Joseph M. Toner. They have spared neither effort nor expense to secure information and can present the work feeling confident of its accuracy in every detail. The authors have been materially assisted in their work by Quartermaster-General Batchelder, U. S. A.; Dr. Toner, Supt. Commerford, of the national cemetery, and others.

CONTENTS.

	PAGE.
CHAPTER I	7

Arlington.

CHAPTER II 14

The founding of Arlington and early life of Custis.

CHAPTER III 28

Custis' life at Arlington—His associates and customs—The Washington relics.

CHAPTER IV 44

Lee at Arlington—Genealogy and early career—His service in the Mexican War.

CHAPTER V 60

Seizure and occupation of Arlington by Federal forces—First interment.

CHAPTER VI 68

Establishment of the National Cemetery—Bodies of soldiers collected on the battle-fields and buried at Arlington.

CHAPTER VII 78

The Government's title to Arlington and how obtained—Interesting legal documents.

CHAPTER VIII 86

The National Cemetery—A general description of Arlington, with an account of some of the distinguished soldiers buried there.

CHAPTER IX 98

Decoration Day and its customs—Some noted orations—Lincoln's Gettysburg address—Ingersoll's prose-poem over the soldier dead.

CHAPTER I.

ARLINGTON.

Arlington. The nation's monument to its immortal dead.

How imposing in its sublimity; how inspiring in its associations. Here, after life's fitful fever, rest thousands of those whose blood was shed that the Union might live.

Historic memories cluster thickly round the name, and it is hallowed by the sacrifices of a nation's homes.

There was scarcely a household but felt the impress of the iron hand of War, and now that Peace has spread her mantle o'er the land, healing the battle scars and bringing reconciliation to the sections, there is scarcely a home in which the thoughts of some within do not turn lovingly to the spot where fathers, brothers, husbands, or sweethearts of the days gone by repose in peaceful slumber. In many a household the empty chair by the fireside still brings tears and heartaches to gray-haired mothers and widowed wives, and to such the intelligence that once again the patriotic men and women of the nation's capital have strewn with flowers the graves of the soldier dead at Arlington comes with a softening touch, easing the reawakened pain and causing hearts to swell with grateful impulse. Still does the grandfather tell the orphan boy how his soldier father served his country well, and then the story, oft repeated, ends in one sad phrase, "he lies at Arlington."

Thus from each section of the land, still sorrowed by the internecine strife, a nation in its sadness turns towards Arlington, and in thought pronounces a benediction o'er the graves. No worthier sepulchre for those who fell in battle could be found. No better monument could be erected to their eternal fame.

This beautiful necropolis of the nation's heroes lies embowered amid the majestic oaks that crown the Virginia hills sweeping away to the south and west of the National Capital. From the portico of the old mansion a panorama is unfolded that is worthy a pilgrimage from the antipodes. To the north, rising back from the river in terraced hills, lies Georgetown, the ancient and honored burg whose wharves once gave welcome to shipping from far distant foreign ports, and whose stately colonial society, tinged with a courtliness bred of constant contact with the English shores, included the oldest and most famous names in our country's history. Here rise the sturdy granite towers of the Georgetown University, bearing proudly the crown of a hundred years of useful existence.

Extending away to the east, in the alluvial basin of the Potomac, lies the National Capital, its imposing structures of marble and granite gleaming in the broad glare of sunlight. To the south, across the sterile, barren plains, rise the spires of Alexandria, while nearer battle-scarred earthworks, silent relics of the great cordon of Union armies that lay around Washington, rear their now peaceful fronts, covered with sod and growths of brush. Every foot of ground for miles around was part of the scene of the great drama of civil war.

The national cemetery lies on the ancient Georgetown and Alexandria pike that a century ago formed a means of communication between these then thriving towns. The land sweeps back in graceful ascent, forming wide, sloping lawns leading up to the graceful structure that crowns the topmost height.

Here every year come thousands to pay their quota of the nation's debt to the dead. Men, women, and children in an endless procession pass through the portals of the national cemetery and, stealing from the bustling world in which they move, spend moments of silent reverence among the dead. No one enters who does not realize more fully than before the heroism of those whose monuments they view, and few there are whose patriotic impulses are not quickened and their sentiments ennobled by a contemplation of the scene presented.

The long rows of white headstones and the imposing shafts of marble and granite that stretch away in picturesque order, on every hand bring recollections of a scene far different, and before the mind passes in review memories of battles fought, where glorious deeds but led to death; where, for the cause they loved, these men gave up their lives. And as these recollections of the past transform the sleeping dead once more into the living heroes, the marble slabs and the inscriptions that they bear change also, and from the sterile name and date that mark each stone appears the record of the soldier's glory.

But not alone does Arlington bring up memories of the war. For fancy, wandering back to days before the civil strife, beholds scenes of homely gayety about the mansion ; sees throngs of men distinguished in their time pass and repass between the columns of the spacious portico, and conjures up a picture of a genial host exercising the truest spirit of hospitality in the days when Virginia was noted alike for the treatment accorded the stranger and the ability of her men.

Not a stone or a tree on the old estate but is associated with recollections of the noblest period of the nation's history. We see the lofty example and precepts of Washington finding later expression in his foster-son, George Washington Parke Custis. About Custis we see assembled at Arlington a band of guests composed of men distinguished in the history of the country. We see the progress of the nation reflected in the personnel of those who wander beneath the forest groves of the old estate.

Lafayette gives place to men like Webster and Henry Clay, and they are in turn succeeded by Lee and those who gathered about that gallant officer before the secession of States brought war between the sections.

The sorrow of a nation, when the death of Custis, the last surviving member of the Mount Vernon household takes place, is shown at Arlington in the assemblage that gathers about his grave, and nowhere does the gloom and sorrow which preceded the civil war settle with stronger effect than at Arlington. We see Lee, flushed with success as a soldier of the Union, struggling between love for his native State and his duty to the Government he had served so well. We see the termination of his career at Arlington in the letter of resignation which he forwards to his old commander. We see the despairing departure from the scenes he loved so well, and find the home that had been bright through generations deserted and buried in gloom.

The scene changes, and we see the forests of the estate leveled, and from every hillside spring white tents peopled by men in warlike garb. We hear the clank of sabre, and the forceful tramp of booted officers echoing through the dismantled rooms of the old house. Earthworks spring up on every side, bristling with guns, and the native silence of the hills are awakened by the blast of bugles and the hoarse tones of command. We mark the progress of the Union forces in the camp life at Arlington. We see the tents that erstwhile sheltered strong and courageous men made now the resting-place of sick and wounded. We see them as they are brought from distant battle-fields and hear their groans, while in and out among them rush the busy surgeons.

Then one by one the yellow mounds come into view to mark the resting-places of the dead. We see them accumulate in number, till thousands upon thousands of those who fell are laid beneath the sod of Arlington. We realize that without preconception or plan the estate has reached its highest destiny in the establishment of a national cemetery. We see it grow in beauty and in grandeur till it becomes a glowing tribute to the valor of those who died in battle, and to it living soldiers look with pride where they, too, will find a worthy sepulchre. We see the nation's most honored heroes laid to rest on the beautiful slope before the mansion, and with swelling hearts watch the pageant that attends these final ceremonies. We see in each recurring year old and young assemble at these graves to deck them with the fairest flowers, and see the outflow of the nation's worthiest sentiment in the pride and care bestowed upon the graves.

To the thousands of visitors to Arlington the spot where stands the grave of Gen. Sheridan is one of greatest interest, and few there are who do not pay their tribute of respect to the worth and courage of so brave an officer.

The ceremonies attending the burial of Sheridan at Arlington were of such an imposing character and were so widely heralded forth to the world through the columns of the press that the incident marks one of the most noted dates in the history of the cemetery.

On the hot August day when the body of Sheridan was borne to the tomb the streets of Washington resounded again to the heavy clatter of cavalry troops, the dull rumbling of guns and caissons, and the marching and countermarching of regiments of infantry in solemn cadence. The long funeral procession passed slowly toward Arlington through the streets of Washington, the waving plumes of the cavalry and the glistening lines of bayonets mingling softly with the fluttering bits of crape that decked helmet and gun-barrel.

The burial services are memorable as being among the most imposing ever witnessed. Thousands gathered on the sloping hillside, surrounding the great hollow square formed by the military escort, and bowed in silent reverence as the brief words of the solemn burial service floated out upon the still air. Many there were who remembered the first burial at Arlington in the days of the war and the contrast was forced home when, as the body was lowered into the grave, the sharp rattling fire of the rifles rang out in successive salutes to the dead leader and hero. Slowly the white smoke lifted and settled among the tree-tops, slowly the vast throng dispersed, and Arlington was left with its immortal dead.

As evening drew on, all evidence of metropolitan life vanished from the solemn scene. A solitary sentinel paced with slow step along the brow of the hill, his feet slashing with a drear, weird sound through the soaked and sodden grass as he passed the newly-made yellow mound standing out in relief against the dull monochrome of the misty gray sky. Overhead a few heavy-winged crows flapped lazily to the nests in the trees below the house, and dark, mysterious bats whirled quickly and silently about through the gloom-stricken trees and darker shadows of the now deserted portico.

Gradually all sight of the city faded from view, and Arlington seemed to withdraw an immeasurable distance from the busy walk of life, and carry its treasured dead with jealous care into the sanctity of the forest primeval. Slowly the heavy, sodden trees seemed to close in upon the grave and its occupant, and long, ghostly shadows fell across it from these guards of nature. The heavy-winged messengers of night flew drowsily along, causing the sentinel ever and anon to start in nervous fear. The drab pillars stood out from the mansion in ghostly relief, and the whole scene was a study in dull gray.

Again, when the great Admiral was laid to rest, vast crowds thronged the hillsides of Arlington and performed the last offices of friendship and admiration. These two, Sheridan and Porter, lie side by side at Arlington and as the dial of inexorable time strikes off the hours of the few remaining great ones of our nation's saddest war, they too will lie on the sloping hillside that looks toward Washington.

This is the Arlington of to-day, rich in memories, hallowed by associations; the mausoleum of the greatest and the bravest; the ast dread assembly ground where meet the rank and file of American valor in brotherly comradeship.

Over the officers who lie at Arlington there are imposing monuments, with lengthy inscriptions setting forth their valorous deeds and praiseworthy achievements. Over the private soldier, who lies with his comrades under long lines of green mounds in regimental array, there is only a small slab, bearing a name and date, with scant room for an epitaph. At every roadside and at every by-path leading into the general sections, however, are tablets bearing an epitaph greater in language and sentiment than the mere empty words of ordinary eulogium.

These are stanzas from the great elegiac poem of Col. Theodore O'Hara:

THE BIVOUAC OF THE DEAD.

The muffled drum's sad roll has beat
  The soldier's last tattoo;
No more on life's parade shall meet
  That brave and fallen few.

On Fame's eternal camping ground
  Their silent tents are spread,
And Glory guards with solemn round
  The bivouac of the dead.

No rumor of the foe's advance
  Now swells upon the wind;
No troubled thought at midnight haunts
  Of loved ones left behind.

No vision of the morrow's strife
  The warrior's dream alarms;
No braying horn nor screaming fife
  At dawn shall call to arms.

The neighing troop, the flashing blade,
  The bugle's stirring blast;
The charge, the dreadful cannonade,
  The din and shout are past.

Rest on, embalmed and sainted dead,
  Dear as the blood ye gave;
No impious footsteps here shall tread
  The herbage of your grave.

Nor shall your glories be forgot
  While Fame her record keeps,
Or Honor points the hallowed spot
  Where Valor proudly sleeps.

Nor wreck, nor change, nor Winter's blight,
  Nor Time's remorseless doom,
Shall dim one ray of holy light
  That gilds your glorious tomb.

CHAPTER II.

THE FOUNDING OF ARLINGTON AND EARLY LIFE OF CUSTIS.

Way back in the early years of the century George Washington Parke Custis, the adopted son of George Washington, built Arlington House and established the estate in which the National Cemetery now stands. It stands as a connecting link between the historic time of struggle, in which the Government was first established, and the later and equally important years of strife that saw the principles for which the colonists fought once more triumphant, and the fabric of Constitutional Government more firmly based upon a federation of loyal States.

With every important epoch in the history of the country Arlington has had its connection. It brings forth recollections of Washington as vividly as phantoms of the past century.

The life of its owner and founder is one of the brightest instances of what a country gentleman of seventy-five years ago could be. It was the home of General Robert E. Lee while he was one of the most distinguished officers of the United States Army, and finally, surrounded by the graves of those immortal heroes of the Civil War, it stands out a monument to American patriotism and courage.

It would be difficult to tell in exactly what connection Arlington appears most interesting, and only by relating its history in what might be termed chronological order can a full appreciation of its historical importance be obtained. It was known and held as an estate by various persons long before the Revolution, having been originally a portion of a grant made by Sir William Berkeley, Governor of Virginia, to Robert Howsen, in 1669. After that it passed into the Alexander family, from which the city of Alexandria took its name, and from the Alexanders it was purchased by John Parke Custis, the son of Martha Washington, and the immediate ancestor of George Washington Parke Custis. It is with the life of the latter that the history of the estate properly begins.

Born and reared under the most remarkable circumstances, and surrounded by all that was best in the way of colonial refinement and culture, George Washington Parke Custis stamped the impress of his own character upon the home he established. The location and architecture of the house indicate culture and refined comfort, while the immensity of the estate, the beauty of the lawns, the broad and well-kept drives, and the ample provision everywhere for the comfort of both man and beast show the indelible traces of the genial and hospitable gentleman.

In many respects the founder of Arlington was a remarkable man. He had good attainments and displayed much originality of thought, and force of expression, both in his writings and speeches, but he was lacking in ambition and accomplished very little.

Over his early training, Washington had exercised the closest supervision. Having devoted all the best years of his own life to the service of his country, the great patriot was anxious that this his adopted son should be so reared that both in the legislative halls and on the field of battle he would be able to serve the Republic, not so much with honor to himself as with profit to the nation. But in Custis, Washington's hopes were never realized. Always a lover of his country, he was willing at any time to take up arms in her defence, but he cared nothing for the turmoil of public life and preferred the soft arts of peace, and the quiet seclusion of his beautiful country home, to the vain search for glory on the tented field, or a factional strife for political supremacy.

The Custis family was one of the oldest in the country at the time of the Revolution, and, in the owner of Arlington, was combined with the Parke family of Virginia. For generations preceding the final separation of the colonies from the mother country, the scions of these two families had distinguished themselves, both at home and abroad, and with each successive achievement had won renown and wealth for themselves, and had added lustre to the fame of colonial chivalry. As early as 1687 we find that a commission was granted Major General John Custis, by Johannes, Lord Howard of Effingham, His Majesty's Lieutenant Governor of Virginia, as collector of customs in certain sections of Virginia. A grandson of this General Custis married the daughter of Daniel Parke and brought about a union of these two leading families.

Daniel Parke was at this time the most distinguished and one of the most remarkable men that the colonies had produced. He was born in Virginia, but passed most of his life in England. He distinguished himself as a soldier, and at the battle of Blenheim served as an aide-de-camp to the Duke of Marlborough. When the great battle had been fought and won, it was Col. Parke that Marlborough selected to bear the tidings to the Queen of England. At the time, such a commission was esteemed a high honor, and it was customary for the Queen to present the bearer of such intelligence with a reward of £500. Col. Parke, however, was a wealthy man, and cared little for money. He requested that instead of a purse the Queen present him with a portrait of herself; this she consented to do, and among the treasures which the Colonel afterwards prized most highly was a painting of Queen Anne, done in miniature and set with diamonds. Col. Parke was afterwards commissioned a general and appointed Governor of the Leeward Islands, a promotion that cost him his life.

An old book now in the possession of the Misses Lee, and for many years on the bookshelves at Arlington, written by George French, contains an account of the administration of Col. Parke at Antigua and of the soldierly manner of his death.

A rebellion had risen in Antigua and Col. Parke had become obnoxious to a seditious faction. Against overpowering odds he waged unsuccessful battle until, driven back to his house, bereft of his command, he found himself, with scarcely a second, in a personal defence. He defied the whole strength of the rebels, however, until at last he received a shot in the thigh, which, though not mortal, disabled him and he fell into the enemy's hands. The story of his death is best told in the graphic words of the homely but thrilling narrative of the ancient chronicler:

"They had now an opportunity to send him away to what place and in what manner they think fit, but instead thereof they use him in the utmost contempt and inhumanity. They strip him of his clothes, kick, spurn at, and beat him with the butts of their muskets, by which means, at last, they break his back. They drag him out into the streets by a leg and arm, and his head trails and beats from step to step of the stone stairs at the entrance of his house, and he is dragged on the coarse gravelly street, which raked the skin from his bones.

"These cruelties and tortures force tears from his eyes, and in this condition he is left expiring, exposed to the scorching sun, out of the heat of which he begs to be removed. The good-natured woman, who, at his request, brought him water to quench his thirst, is threatened by one Samuel Watkins to have a sword passed through her for her humanity, and the water is dashed out of her hands.

"He is insulted and reviled by every scoundrel, in the agonies of death, but makes no other return but these mild expressions: 'Gentlemen, if you have no sense of honor left, pray have some of humanity.' He gratefully owns the kindness of friends and prays God to reward those who stood by him that day. At last he was removed into the house of one Mr. John Wright, near the place where he lay, and there recommending his soul to God with some pious ejaculations, he pays the great debt of nature, and death, less cruel than his enemies, put a period to his sufferings.

"After they had surfeited themselves with cruelties, they plundered the General's house and broke open his storehouses, so that his estate must have suffered by that day in money, plate, jewels, and household goods, by the most moderate computation, five thousand pounds sterling, for which his executors have obtained no satisfaction to this day. Thus died Col. Parke, whose brave end shows him sufficiently deserving of the commission he bore, and by his death acquired an honor to his memory which the base aspersions of his enemies could not overthrow."

This tragedy occurred on the 7th of December, 1810. But while Col. Parke was chasing the bubble reputation at the cannon's mouth, Mrs. Parke was engaged in Virginia in rearing three beautiful and accomplished daughters. In his letters to his wife, Col. Parke assured her that his heart was in Virginia, but a prolonged absence from that highly important organ seems to have had but little effect on the gallant Colonel, as his conduct shows that he much preferred the fascinations of court life and the excitement of battle to the society of his own wife and daughters. They got along well enough without him, however, and the three girls grew into handsome young women, such as the Colonel himself would have been proud of.

The eldest one, Frances, was a proud and haughty beauty, for whom a number of young Virginia gentlemen were sighing. Among the number was Col. John Custis.

Col. Custis was wealthy and occupied an influential position in the colonies. With these factors in his favor he was able to carry off the prize, and Miss Frances Parke became Mrs. John Custis.

The couple went to live on Col. Custis' estate on the eastern shore of Virginia, which they called Arlington, in honor of the Earl of Arlington, to whom Charles the Second had made extensive grants in the Old Dominion. Mrs. Custis, while she had inherited a goodly portion of beauty from both her parents, had also inherited from her father some of his sterner qualities, and Custis was not long in finding out that, with him, marriage had been a failure. The union proved anything but a happy one, and only the death of the lady put an end to their domestic infelicity. As a result of his unhappy married life, Col. Custis had placed, at his death, an inscription on his tombstone which clearly shows his estimation of his wife. The inscription has been frequently published before, but is so remarkable that it is here reproduced.

> Under this marble tomb lies the body
> of the Hon. JOHN CUSTIS, Esq.,
> of the city of Williamsburg
> and parish of Bruton,
> formerly of Hengar's parish, on the
> Eastern Shore
> of Virginia and County of Northampton,
> aged 71 years, and yet lived but seven years,
> which was the space of time he kept
> a bachelor's home at Arlington,
> on the Eastern shore of Virginia.

This monument was erected on his estate at Arlington, and was standing until a few years ago.

Two children were the result of this marriage, a son, Daniel Parke Custis, and a daughter, Fannie Parke Custis. The latter married a Capt. Dausie, against her father's wishes, and was never afterwards recognized by her family. The son, Daniel, married the beautiful Martha Dandridge, afterwards the wife of Gen. George Washington. It was from this union that John Parke Custis, the father of the philosopher of Arlington. sprung The marriage of young Custis and Martha Dandridge was one of the big social event of colonial times. The young lad had been the reigning belle at Williamsburg, where the royal governors of the colony held their court, and her marriage attracted the attention of the entire official circle.

After their marriage they went to live at what was then the seat of the Custises, on the banks of the Pamunkey, where their union was blessed with four children, Daniel Parke, Fannie Parke, John Parke, and Martha Parke. The two oldest children died very young, and at the age of thirty their father also died, leaving Mrs. Custis a young widow, with two small children.

She was wealthy, having come into possession of all the Custis estates, and handsome, and when her period of mourning for the late Mr. Custis had expired, became once more as attractive to suitors as she had been before her marriage. It was therefore not long before the cavaliers of the Old Dominion once more "came a-wooing" to the home of the beautiful Custis widow.

There was among them a young and distinguished officer of the colonial service, who had already attracted attention, both by his courage and brilliant abilities as a soldier, and his sterling qualities of mind and character. Except for these qualities, however, the gentleman was little distinguished either by wealth or influence, but this fact had small weight with the beautiful widow, and she was soon persuaded to cast off her weeds to become the wife of Col. George Washington.

Of the happiness of this union, the constant devotion of one to the other, and the perfection of domestic bliss which their home lives at Mt. Vernon attained, it is not the purpose of this volume to treat.

The importance of the union so far as this work is concerned lies in the fact that by the marriage of Washington and the Widow Custis the former became the guardian and natural protector of John Parke Custis, the head of the Custis family.

The two children, John and Martha Custis, were still quite young when their mother became Mrs. Washington. They were taken to Mount Vernon, and for several years spent the happy hours of their childhood playing about the lawns that slope from the historic old mansion down to the Potomac.

Of Martha little need be said. In what little was written about her by contemporaneous historians, she is described as being a handsome, but exceedingly dark brunette. She had a great affection for her stepfather, and he regarded her with all the feeling of pride and affection that a man could bestow upon his own child. Her life, however, was a brief one, and at the age of sixteen she died at Mount Vernon. All her fortune, which she had inherited from her father, she bequeathed to Washington.

John Parke Custis, the other child, was a sturdy youth on whom Mrs. Washington, after the death of her daughter, centered all her affections, and in whom Washington took a deep interest. Washington was exceedingly anxious that he should receive a thorough education, and with this end in view placed him under the care of an Episcopal clergyman at Annapolis, in Maryland. Young Custis, however, had little liking for study, and finding the restraint of the good clergyman, with whom he lodged, of the mildest form, he spent a great portion of his time in hunting, and in other pursuits, a taste for which he had inherited from his hearty and adventurous ancestors. Tiring altogether of his books, he conceived a passionate desire to travel, but in this he found himself opposed by the indomitable will of Washington.

It is almost unnecessary to say that in a conflict between the two the inflexible determination of Washington prevailed, and young Custis was sent back to his books.

But Custis was not a youth who could be totally suppressed, even by the conqueror of British armies, and before very long he had found a new diversion from his studies and had become engaged to Eleanor Calvert, the second daughter of Benedict Calvert, of Mt. Airy, Maryland, a direct descendant from Lord Baltimore. Custis was then about eighteen years of age and the news of his engagement, which Washington regarded as another youthful escapade, was received by that gentleman with great displeasure. He did nothing, however, to prevent the union, but on the other hand wrote to the young lady's father, suggesting that the engagement be continued, but insisting that the marriage be deferred until Custis had completed his education.

It was accordingly agreed that the youth should spend two years at Kings College, now Columbia College, New York, and he was sent there to continue his studies.

He remained at college but a few months, however, and then, despite the opposition of the elders on both sides, married Miss

Calvert on the 3d of February, 1774, when little more than nineteen years of age.

Custis took his youthful bride to Abbingdon, an estate not far from Alexandria, where four children were born to them. These were Elizabeth Parke, who afterwards married Mr. Law, a nephew of Lord Ellenborough; Martha Parke, who was married early to Thomas Peter; Eleanor Parke, who married Lawrence Lewis, a nephew of Washington, and George Washington Parke Custis, the owner of the Arlington estate.

With the beginning of the Revolutionary War, John Parke Custis promptly offered his services to his country and served with distinction through all the battles, as an aide to General Washington. His death was brought about by camp fever, which he contracted during the siege of Yorktown. The disease attacked him very violently, just as the siege was about to end. He realized that it would terminate fatally, but insisted on remaining in camp to witness the surrender of Cornwallis. He was supported by his attendants to the place where the surrender took place, and after he had seen the sword of the British commander turned over to Washington, was removed to Eltham, a country place not far distant. Washington followed him hastily the same evening, but arrived at Eltham only a short time before his death. Mrs. Custis was present when her husband expired, and as she stood beside his death-bed, weeping bitterly, Washington clasped her tenderly in his arms and said, "From this moment I adopt his two youngest children as my own."

In this manner George Washington Parke Custis and his sister Eleanor became the children of the first President, and their childhood was inseparably connected with the home life at Mount Vernon.

George Washington Parke Custis was but six months old when the death of his father left him to the care of General Washington. From that time to the death of Washington himself, his life was spent principally at the home of the great patriot, sometimes at Mount Vernon and a portion of the time in the household of the President at New York and Philadelphia.

The war in which the colonies had been plunged ended shortly after his birth, and it was with scenes of peace and rapidly extending prosperity that his earliest recollections were associated. He was eight years of age when, in 1789, Washington was inaugurated the first President of the United States. Previous to this, the boy had played games with Lafayette and the other heroes of the Revolution, upon the lawns of Mount Vernon, and was as well acquainted with all the prominent men of the time as a boy could be. They were, in fact, about his only playfellows, and if not romping with them he was toddling along by the side of his foster parent, listening with precocious gravity to some discussion Washington was having with one of his numerous and distinguished visitors.

When Washington moved to New York, as President of the United States, little Custis and his sister Eleanor were taken along and became a part of the Presidential household, in the old Osgood house, on Cherry street. Of his surroundings and associations during the eventful years he spent there, an idea can be best obtained from his own description of the Washington household, given in his memoirs of Washington. These were published after his death by his daughter, Mrs. Robert E. Lee, and can now be found only in a few of the more complete libraries of the country.

"His domestic family," Mr. Custis says, speaking of President Washington, "consisted of Mrs. Washington, the two adopted children, Mr. Lear, Colonel Humphreys, and Messrs. Nelson and Lewis, secretaries, and Major William Jackson, aide-de-camp.

"Persons visiting the house in Cherry street at this time will wonder how a building so small could contain the many and mighty spirits that thronged it. Congress, Cabinet, all public functionaries in the commencement of the Government, were selected from the very élite of the nation. Pure patriotism, commanding talent, eminent services, were the proud and indispensable requisites for official station in the first days of the Republic.

"The first Congress was a most enlightened and dignified body. In the Senate were several members of the Congress of 1776, and signers of the Declaration of Independence—Richard Henry Lee, who moved the Declaration, John Adams, who seconded it, with Sherman, Morris, Carroll, and others.

"The levees of the first President were attended by these illustrious men and by many others of the patriots, statesmen, and soldiers, who could say of the Revolution, "*Magna pars fui*," while numbers of foreigners and strangers of distinction crowded to the seat of the General Government, all anxious to witness the grand experiment that was to determine how much rational liberty mankind is capable of enjoying, without that liberty degenerating into licentiousness.

"Mrs. Washington's drawing-rooms on Friday nights were attended by the grace and beauty of New York. The President himself was always present, and about him gathered the most distinguished of the Revolutionary heroes."

Amid such scenes and with such surroundings young Custis grew to manhood. He had constantly before him as a guide to his conduct and habits of thought the lofty example of Washington and his compatriots, while over his studies and pleasures Washington exercised a careful and a fatherly supervision. The idol of his grandmother and the hope of his foster father, the restraint placed upon him by his guardians was only that which might save him from habits of dissipation, or licentious association. It was small wonder, then, that the boy should reach his early manhood with the loftiest ideas of honor and propriety of conduct. His unswerving integrity was almost as marked as that of Washington himself. He abhorred the licentious vices of other young men of his age, while his patriotism and generosity, which he breathed in with the atmosphere in which he lived, were manifest in his character throughout his entire life.

But though Custis was in the matter of virtue and sentiment a credit to his friends, he was woefully lacking in firmness and in energy. The term *dillettante* describes his character exactly. He had some knowledge of art, and at his home in Arlington painted a number of pictures, principally of battle scenes, with Washington as the central figure. He was a graceful and forcible writer, but his literary works consist only of an imperfect series of papers on Washington, some fragmentary poems, and a few poor dramas. He was an orator capable of rare eloquence, but he never used this ability save at a few funerals or on some occasion where the duty of welcoming a guest or of praising a friend devolved upon him. Even as a farmer he was a theorist and a dreamer, and though he made numerous wise efforts to improve the agricultural methods of his time, his weakness of purpose and lack of ambition rendered these endeavors abortive. But with all this,

his character stands out, in the early history of the century, with great prominence, as that of a genial and accomplished gentleman, simple and modest in demeanor, unswerving in his integrity and friendships, a lover of all that was best in his fellow-men and in the institutions of his country. He was such a man as historians ignore but mankind bestows its reverence and affection upon.

The weakness in the character of Custis was very apparent to Washington and caused him great anxiety and disappointment. "He had a tear, for we have seen it shed with parental solicitude over the manifold errors and follies of our unworthy youth," says Custis himself, in treating of the character of Washington, but the tears shed by the General were due entirely to his own disappointment. He had very ambitious hopes for his adopted son, and it was with bitter regret that he saw they could never be realized. Custis cared nothing for the allurements of public life. He never conceived the idea that there was any likelihood his country would need his services as a statesman, and while he entered, as a student, into Washington's schemes for his future welfare with good-natured complaisance, he never made the slightest effort to bring about their success.

Custis' early education he received from tutors at Mount Vernon, but when he was fifteen years of age he was sent to Princeton College, and while there he was constantly receiving letters from Washington urging him to attend closely to his studies, and finding fault at times with the younger man's slow progress. The correspondence between Washington and young Custis at this period is of considerable interest. Custis is constantly veiling excuses for his own idleness under expressions of the warmest admiration and affection for Washington. He addresses his foster father in terms that must have seemed to the elder man pedantic and affected; for in his replies Washington pays no attention to the well-meant flattery which Custis' letters contain, but shows clearly that he fully understands the youth's subterfuges and takes no care to conceal the anger they cause him.

In a letter written from Philadelphia in 1796, he says to Custis:

"You are now extending into that stage of life when good or

bad habits are formed; when the mind will be turned to things useful and praiseworthy, or to dissipation and vice. Fix on whichever it may, it will stick by you; for you know it has been truly said 'that as the twig is bent so it will grow.' This, in a strong point of view, shows the propriety of letting your inexperience be directed by maturer advice, and in placing guard upon the avenues which lead to idleness and vice. The latter will approach like a thief, working upon your passions, encouraged, perhaps, by bad examples, the propensity to which will increase in proportion to the practice of it and your yielding.

"This admonition proceeds from the purest affection for you; but I do not mean by it that you are to become a stoic, or to deprive yourself in the intervals of study of any recreations or manly exercises which reason approves.

"'Tis well to be on good terms with all your fellow-students, and I am pleased to hear you are so; but while a courteous behavior is due to all, select the most deserving only for your friendships, and before this becomes intimate weigh their dispositions and characters well.

"True friendship is a plant of slow growth; to be sincere there must be a congeniality of temper and pursuits. Virtue and vice cannot be allied, nor can idleness and industry.

"Of course, if you resolve to adhere to the two former of these extremes, an intimacy with those who incline to the latter of them would be extremely embarrassing to you; it would be a stumbling-block in your way, and act like a millstone hung to your neck, for it is the nature of idleness and vice to obtain as many votaries as they can. I would guard you, too, against imbibing hasty and unfavorable impressions of any one. Let your judgment always balance well before you decide; and even then where there is no occasion for expressing an opinion it is best to be silent, for there is nothing more certain than that it is at all times more easy to make enemies than friends. And besides, to speak evil of any one, unless there is unequivocal proof of their deserving it, is an injury for which there is no adequate reparation. For, as Shakespeare says, 'He that robs me of my good name enriches not himself, but renders me poor indeed.'"

There are a number of other letters showing the fatherly solicitude of Washington for Custis' welfare, all couched in a tone of mild reproof. As the years pass, the reproof becomes more pronounced until it closely resembles fault-finding. For, in spite of all that Washington could do or say, Custis was willing only to do the work he found most agreeable, and his reading was of a desultory character, such as his own inclinations led to.

The young man was transferred from Princeton to Annapolis, where he continued his studies under the direction of Mr. McDowell, president of Annapolis College. Washington, in a letter to that gentleman, in 1798, gives an estimate of Custis' character and ability which is here valuable. He says, after explaining that a fever had prevented his writing earlier:

"Were the case otherwise, I should, I confess, be at a loss to point out any precise course of study for Mr. Custis. My views regarding him have already been made known to you, and therefore it is not necessary to repeat them on this occasion. It is not merely the best course for him to pursue that requires a consideration, but such an one as he can be induced to pursue and will contribute to his improvement and the object in view. In directing the first of these objects, a gentleman of your literary discernment and knowledge of the world would be at no loss, without any suggestion of mine, if there was as good a disposition to receive as there are talents to acquire knowledge; but as there seems to be in this youth an inconquerable indolence of temper and a dereliction, in fact, to all study, it must rest with you to lead him in the best manner, and by the easiest modes you can devise, to the study of such useful acquirements as may be serviceable to himself and eventually beneficial to his country."

Almost immediately after the date of this letter Custis left college at Annapolis and was permitted by Washington to continue his studies with a tutor at Mount Vernon.

About this time he was appointed a cornet of horse in the army and soon afterwards was promoted to the position of aide-de-camp to Gen. Charles Cotesworth Pinckney, of South Carolina, with the rank of colonel. A few months afterwards the death of Washington occurred, and this event had a marked effect upon young Custis' character and after-life.

He was sincerely attached to his foster-father and never lost the feeling of extreme admiration and reverence with which Washington had inspired him. But, with the latter's death, all the ambitious plans for Custis' advancement vanished into thin air, and the young man became the good-natured and indolent gentleman of refined tastes such as we find him years afterwards at Arlington. Washington's confidence in him is shown by the fact that in his will he made him one of the executors of his estate.

CHAPTER III.

CUSTIS' LIFE AT ARLINGTON—HIS ASSOCIATES AND CUSTOMS—THE WASHINGTON RELICS.

The death of Washington caused no immediate change in the domestic circle at Mount Vernon. Mrs. Washington continued to live at the old homestead, and her grandson remained with her. At Mrs. Washington's death, two years later, however, the estate passed to other members of the Washington family, and Custis took up his residence at Arlington.

At this time Custis was a very wealthy man. He had just reached his 21st birthday and had succeeded to all the Custis estates left by his father. They consisted of extensive and fertile plantations in Westmoreland county and along the Pamunkey river, and the Arlington estate, embracing about 1,100 acres, which his father, John Custis, as already stated, had purchased from the Alexanders. In addition he inherited from Washington a tract of 1,200 acres of land lying north of Arlington, in Fairfax county. He possessed a large number of slaves, a great many horses, used in the cultivation of his estates, and other forms of property.

It was the magnificent location of the Arlington estate that caused Custis to select it, from among his other possessions, as his home. The Capital of the Nation had already been moved to Washington, and the growth of the magnificent federal city was making fair progress. Within sight of the Capitol building and overlooking the beautiful river, with which Custis had been familiar from his earliest childhood, no better site for a future home could possibly have been selected. It was contiguous to the country about Mt. Vernon, endeared to him by so many valued associations, and within easy reaching distance of Alexandria, then a centre for the wealth and fashion of the Old Dominion.

But the Arlington on which Custis took up his residence then bore no resemblance in appearance to the Arlington of his later The estate consisted chiefly of woodland, with but a few hundred acres of cleared land lying below the hills, on the banks of the river. In this cleared space stood the manor house, an unpretentious dwelling containing only four rooms. It was located near the bank of what was called the Little River, about a mile to the eastward of the present mansion, and was surrounded by a grove of magnificent oaks. Not far below it was the famous Custis Spring, about which so much has been written. The crumbling walls of the old mansion still stand to mark the spot on which it stood, and until the occupation of the estate by the Federal forces, it was in a fair state of preservation. Within a few years, however, the building has been almost completely demolished by direction of the War Department, for what purpose no one has yet been able to determine.

The house was a very old one, having been erected by the Alexanders in the early part of the 18th century, long before the old house at Mount Vernon had been thought of. Had it been treated by the Government with the respect which the antiquity of its origin merited it would be now one of the most interesting relics of the early history of the country. But the War Department had little more use for the old mansion as a relic than did Custis as a place of residence. It was with him but a temporary abode, and within a year of his leaving Mount Vernon he began the erection of the splendid "Arlington House," which, from its present condition, would seem to have been built for all time as a monument to its founder.

Mr. Custis, in selecting the site for his house, showed clearly his appreciation of the beautiful, and his artistic tastes and broad mental visions are manifest in the structure which he designed and erected.

The tall massive columns of the portico are designed from the most perfect type of Greek architecture, while the broad hallways and spacious chambers are indicative, even in their present dismantled condition, of wholesome comfort and homely elegance.

The house is modeled after the ancient Temple of Theseus at Athens, but in adopting this design Mr. Custis only followed a custom that prevailed throughout the South, and, indeed, in some parts of New England, in the early part of the century. In building his house, Mr. Custis, however, brought the style to a higher state of perfection than it had attained before, and

"Arlington House" was known from the time of its erection till the breaking out of the war as the finest specimen of the landed proprietor's residence that could be found within the limits of the slave States.

It was built of brick, and stuccoed, and the material for its construction was produced on the grounds about it. Brick-yards were established on a portion of the estate, now part of Fort Myer, where the bricks were burned under Mr. Custis' own supervision.

Just about the time the Arlington Mansion was completed Mr. Custis married Mary Lee Fitzhugh, the daughter of Fitzhugh of Chatham, near Fredericksburg. He was then but twenty-three years of age, while his wife was but sixteen. He took his bride to Arlington at once, and there, for the next fifty years, they lived a life of the most delightful contentment, surrounded constantly by relatives and guests.

With the generous hospitality of a wealthy Virginia planter, Mr. Custis entertained lavishly. All the old revolutionary heroes were welcome guests at his board, while the distinguished men of a succeeding generation delighted in visiting the hospitable farmer.

Once comfortably settled with his bride in their new and magficent home, Mr. Custis gave his attention to improving the agricultural methods of the time. In 1803 Col. David Humphreys returned from a mission to Spain, bringing with him one hundred fine-wooled Merino sheep.

Custis took a great interest in the matter of stock breeding and domestic manufactures, and he saw in the advent of the Merinos a promise of the opening, in America, of woolen cloth making. At that time all the cloth of this character used in the country was imported from England, and could only be obtained at considerable cost. The importance of the matter, because of the success of the manufacture of cotton cloth by the Southern States, was occupying then the thoughts of a number of public-spirited men.

To foster improvements in sheep and to encourage woolen manufacture at home, Mr. Custis, in 1803, called a convention of those interested in sheep husbandry and wool manufacture. It met at Arlington House and really marked the beginning of the woolen-manufacturing interests of the country. It is not known whether or not this convention recommended the imposition by Congress of a tariff on woolen goods, but from the views held at that time regarding, and the actual needs of, an infant industry, it is presumed it did. The convention also led to the adoption by Mr. Custis of a custom which rendered his fine estate and himself famous throughout the country. He entered into sheep-raising with considerable ardor, and in succeeding years the annual sheep-shearing at Arlington Spring brought together from all parts of the country an assemblage of men interested in the industry, and others distinguished by their ability in public life. All were the guests of Mr. Custis, and the occasion became almost an annual festival.

The spring at which the gatherings took place was at the foot of a wooded slope, near the bank of the river and not far from where stood the old Alexander mansion. It was a pure and copious fountain, gushing out from the roots of a huge and venerable oak tree, which doubtless stood there when the Indians of a former age came thither to slake their thirst. Around the spring a beautiful grassy lawn, shaded by a variety of trees, extended, affording a magnificent resort for such meetings. Mr. Custis always presided. Toasts were drunk, speeches were made, and prizes were awarded by Mr. Custis to the persons bringing, for purposes of exhibition, the finest specimens of sheep. Generally these ceremonies took place under the shelter of Washington's war tent, which was brought out for the occasion from among the treasured relics of the first President that Mr. Custis possessed.

The host usually made a stirring address, and in one of his speeches, delivered while wool manufactures were yet unknown in America, he said prophetically: " America shall be great and free and minister to her own wants by the employment of her own resources. The citizens of my country will proudly appear when clothed in the produce of their own native soil."

The efforts Mr. Custis was making in behalf of the sheep-raising industry attracted general attention, and among his letters of that time we find several from James Madison, then Secretary of State, and afterwards President of the United States.

In one of these Mr. Custis is informed that Mr. Madison "offers for himself the thanks to which Mr. Custis is entitled from his fellow-citizens for his laudable and encouraging efforts to increase and improve an animal which contributes a material so precious to the independent comfort and prosperity of our country. Mr. Madison wishes that Mr. Custis may be amply gratified in the success of his improving experiments, and that his patriotic example may find as many followers as it merits."

In another letter on the same subject, Mr. Madison says : " It gives me pleasure to find your attention to this interesting subject does not relax, and that you are successfully inviting to it other public-spirited gentlemen."

In this matter, however, like in a good many others, Mr. Custis understood the theory of sheep-raising and of arousing interest in the subject better than he did the practice. His own efforts met with very poor success. He established a large flock of Merinos on the hills of Arlington, but they were gradually killed off by thieves and dogs, until but two animals remained to show that Mr. Custis was still true to his principles.

The absence of the sheep somewhat interfered with the successful continuation of the annual sheep-shearing gatherings at the Custis spring and they were eventually abandoned.

Mr. Custis retained his interest in sheep-raising, however, and before his own flock became extinct he had the satisfaction of seeing the manufacture of American woolens grow into an important industry. He also maintained a broad and deep interest in all other agricultural pursuits, and for a great many years he was an active member and one of the vice-presidents of the American Agricultural Society.

When the war of 1812 occurred Mr. Custis served as a volunteer to oppose the British when they entered Maryland and ascended the Potomac to attack the Capital. He fought in the battle of North Point as a private soldier. After the war he refused to accept any compensation for his services, but rendered assistance to his less wealthy companions in arms in prosecuting legitimate claims against the Government.

During these earlier years of the century Mr. Custis was widely known as the adopted child of George Washington, and as the character of that soldier and statesman was better understood and appreciated by the generation that succeeded his, as the years passed, Mr. Custis became more and more an object of re-

spect and veneration. His own character, too, entitled him to the
utmost consideration from his contemporaries. He was sought
after as a public speaker; invitations to his home at Arlington
were coveted by the leading men of the time, and his friendship
was cherished by all he bestowed it upon. Congress invited him
to deliver an address to a joint assemblage of the two houses on
the character of his foster-father, and everywhere he was accorded
the utmost respect and consideration.

A number of Mr. Custis' speeches were preserved by his relatives, and they show him to have been a speaker of marked ability and eloquence. An address he delivered on the death of General Lingan is still admired by readers, and another speech, which he delivered on the overthrow of Napoleon, called forth the most graceful acknowledgments from the representative of Russia at Washington, and from other foreign ministers.

When Lafayette revisited the United States in 1824, among his first visits was one to Mr. Custis. During Lafayette's exile from France, his son, George Washington Lafayette, had lived for a period of several months with Washington at Mount Vernon. There he had formed a strong attachment for young Custis, and the two renewed their friendship on this occasion with the utmost warmth. Lafayette spent much time with Mr. Custis, and enriched, during his stay, the latter's fund of information concerning Washington, from his own reminiscences of his old commander. Together they visited the tomb of Washington, where, beside the last resting-place of the country's greatest hero, Mr. Custis presented the illustrious Frenchman with a ring, in which was some of the hair of the dead chieftain. The following account of the visit was found by the authors in the files of the old National Intelligencer, and was published in that paper immediately after the occurrence, on the 26th of October, 1824:

"The solemn and imposing scene of the visit of Lafayette to the tomb of Washington took place on Sunday, the 17th of October, 1824. About 1 o'clock the General left the steamboat *Petersburg*, at anchor off Mount Vernon, and was received into a barge manned and steered by captains of vessels from Alexandria, who had handsomely volunteered their services for this interesting occasion. He was accompanied in the barge by his family and suite, and Mr. Secretary John C. Calhoun. On reaching the shores he was received by Mr. Lawrence Lewis, the nephew of Washington, and by the gentlemen of the family of Judge Bushrod Washington (the Judge himself being absent on official duties), and conducted to the ancient mansion, where, forty years before, Lafayette took the last leave of his 'hero, his friend, and our country's preserver.'

"After remaining a few minutes in the house the General proceeded to the vault, supported by Mr. Lewis and the gentlemen relatives of the Judge, and accompanied by G. W. Lafayette and G. W. P. Custis, the children of Mt. Vernon, both having shared the paternal care of the great chief. Mr. Custis wore the ring suspended from a Cincinnati ribbon. Arrived at the sepulchre, after a pause, Mr. Custis addressed the General as follows:

* * * * * *

"The General, having received the ring, pressed it to his bosom and replied:

"'The feelings which at this awful moment oppress my heart do not leave the power of utterance. I can only thank you, my dear Custis, for your precious gift and pay a silent homage to the tomb of the greatest and best of men, my paternal friend.'

"The General affectionately embraced the donor and the other three gentlemen, and gazing intently on the receptacle of departed greatness, fervently pressed his lips to the door of the vault, while tears filled the furrows of the veteran's cheeks. The key was now applied to the lock, the door flew open and discovered the coffins strewn with flowers and with evergreens. The General descended the steps and kissed the leaden cells which contained the ashes of the great chief and his venerable consort, and then retired in an excess of feeling which language is too poor to describe. After partaking of refreshments at the house and making a slight tour of the grounds, the General returned to the shore. In descending the hill to the river the horses became restive. Some spirited young men rushed forward, removed them from the carriage and would have drawn the vehicle themselves. But this the General would not permit, and, alighting, he walked to the shore, a distance of about a quarter of a mile.

"Previous to re-embarkation, Mr. Custis presented the Cincinnati ribbon, which had borne the ring to the vault, to Major Ewell, a veteran of the Revolution, requesting him to take part of it and divide the remainder among the young men present, which was done, and a general struggle ensued for the smallest portion of it. The same barge conveyed the General to the *Petersburg*, the Marine Band playing, as before, a strain of solemn music. The vessel immediately proceeded on her voyage to Yorktown. Not a soul intruded upon the privacy of the visit to the tomb. Nothing occurred to disturb its reverential solemnity. The old oaks which grew around the sepulchre, touched with the mellow lustre of autumn, appeared rich and ripe as the autumnal honors of Lafayette. Not a murmur was heard save the strains of solemn music and the deep and measured sound of artillery, which awoke the echoes around the hallowed heights of Mount Vernon.

" 'Tis done! The greatest and most affecting scene of the grand drama has closed, and the pilgrim who now repairs to the tomb of the Father of his Country will find its laurels moistened by the tears of Lafayette."

Mr. Custis never, as already intimated, cut much of a figure as a public man. Most of the public gatherings in which he took an active part, such as the sheep-raisers' convention, and kindred meetings, were held at Arlington, where he appeared more in the character of a host than of an individual endeavoring to affect public opinion or public events. He spent most of his time at home, and there he delighted to play the host to whoever came his way. He cared not whether the wayfarer that entered his grounds was shabbily dressed, or arrayed in purple and fine linen. One was as welcome as the other, and neither was allowed to depart until he had feasted with his host and pledged his health in a glass of something invigorating. Prohibitionists were scarce in those days, although temperance was the rule and not the exception among the better classes, so that Mr. Custis' kindly entertainment of the stranger at his gates did not call forth the storm of public condemnation that it would now. But indeed Custis would have cared little if it had. In his home life he cared about as much for what his neighbors and the good gossips among them might say concerning him as did the early American savages for the tracts sent them by the well-intending missionary societies of the mother country.

He had very well-defined principles of his own, and if he lived up to them he was satisfied. It was one of his customs to attend the inauguration of each succeeding President from the time of Washington until 1857. But except when some such state occasion took him to the Capital his visits to Washington were not frequent. After the visit of Lafayette his public appearances became few and far between. He was then a middle-aged man, and his home life, surrounded as it was with so much that brought to him recollections of a glorious past, was all that he desired.

He was at this time a sturdy man, though slightly built. The promise of personal beauty which his early youth had given was not exactly fulfilled in his maturer years. His features were sharp and irregular, his nose long and thin, his forehead low and receding, his hair was light and thin, and in after years his head was bald. A firmly set mouth and a well-rounded chin were his best features, and indicated a firmness of character which his light-blue and rather weak eyes seemed to contradict. His cheeks were slightly sunken and gave to his face a somewhat cadaverous appearance, which was hardly improved by the thin side-whiskers he wore. He was careless with his dress, and the visitor to Arlington was often surprised at the shabby-appearing gentleman who appeared to welcome him to so splendid a mansion.

Mr. Custis was a great hunter, and in his out-of-doors life he was generally accompanied by his gun and his dogs. There was plenty of game on the Arlington hills, and Mr. Custis combined the work of superintending the operations of his numerous slaves with the pleasure of hunting. He was a good shot and tireless when in pursuit of game. None of the younger men, in fact, could keep pace with him, and he often amused himself, when hunting with a party of his guests, by tiring them all out, though most of them were his juniors by a number of years. On these occasions, and they were generally such as remained in the memories of those who participated in the expeditions as very pleasant recollections, the day generally wound up with a banquet at the house of the host and an evening of delightful gaiety. When the company would assemble around the banquet table, Mr. Custis delighted in making merry over the fatigue experienced by his guests during the day. He would pretend that he himself was but a shadow of his former self, and would relate stories of his early youth, and of the prowess of the men that won the revolutionary battles, that made his guests smile incredulously. Of course, none of this good-natured raillery was meant by the genial host, and as his guests recognized its insincerity they laughed with him at their own expense and discomfiture.

Mr. Custis at this time conducted his estates on a system that was almost like the governing of a small principality. The Arlington estate was his home, and upon it he did very little farming for profit. His income he derived from what he called his farms in Westmoreland county. The Arlington estate was simply his private grounds, and its cultivation at all was for the purpose of providing for the numerous slaves that he kept about him. In his treatment of his negroes, Mr. Custis was as considerate as he was regarding any other class of human beings, and the glaring evils of slavery were never apparent upon his property. Each slave had a house apportioned him, and a bit of ground, the produce of which he owned as securely as if his title to the land he occupied was duly recorded in the records of the county courts.

The slaves were of course compelled to give a good portion of their time to the master's service, but their work was not hard and they were liberally provided for in decrepit old age as well as in sturdy youth. Mr. Custis also respected the domestic relations of the negroes, and the separation of mothers from their children and of wives from their husbands was a practice in which he never indulged himself, and which he abhorred in others. As a result his slaves were devoted to him. He was not only a kind master, but was their friend, and delighted as much in joking with them, and in making harmless fun of them, as he did in the conversations of his neighbors. Active both in mental and physical exercise, Mr. Custis' out-door life at Arlington was at once to him a source of pleasurable recreation and of physical health and vigor.

His in-door life was equally admirable. To judge of the home he occupied, one must picture the now bare and desolate rooms of the fine old mansion filled with the handsome furniture of a hundred years ago, the walls resplendent with art treasures, and the whole house glowing with life and comfort. Through the open windows the scent of flowers is wafted in on the summer breezes. Flowers grace the tables and ornament the mantelpieces, and on every side are evidences of wealth, culture, and housewifely taste. The rooms are filled with Mr. Custis' guests, and bustling about, in obedience to instructions given, are numerous black-faced servants, all neatly dressed, and all proud of the master they serve. The central figure in this goodly assemblage is the host, courteous and considerate to all. His anecdotes are the best that are told, his views on all topics are listened to with respect, and his regard is desired by everyone about him.

Mr. Custis' home life was not constantly spent, however, in entertaining his guests. He had his hours for work, and spent them in his library, where he engaged himself either with his incompleted literary efforts or with his attempted reproductions in oil of revolutionary scenes and figures. He read a great deal, but his reading was done generally at times when Arlington was deserted by guests. When there were people about to enjoy themselves Mr. Custis preferred being among them, and really got more enjoyment out of the pleasures of others than he did from any other source of amusement.

About the famous Arlington spring he constructed several buildings, among others a big kitchen and dining-room and a dancing pavilion, and these, with the beautiful grounds about them, he threw open to the picnic parties from Washington, Georgetown, and the country around. He built a wharf out into the river, and induced a small steamer, called the G. W. P. Custis, to make several trips daily to the spring.

The spring at once became the most attractive spot in that section of the country, and a throng of people visited it daily. No intoxicating liquors were permitted on the premises, but, except in this particular, the visitors were entirely free from restraint, and could go and come as they pleased. All Mr. Custis asked in return for his hospitality was the observance by his guests of the moral principles he upheld himself and a reciprocation of the kindly feeling that animated him.

Every day during the pleasant weather Mr. Custis joined the merry-makers at the spring and frequently joined in the games of the children and the youthful people. Often he took with him his violin—for, with his other accomplishments, Mr. Custis was also something of a musician—and never were the dances so enjoyed or the fun gayer than when the host furnished the music with his own bow.

These gatherings continued during every summer from the time of their commencement to the death of Mr. Custis, in 1857, and their popularity constantly increased. After Mr. Custis' death they ceased, the spring was abandoned, and now no vestige of the green lawns that were the scenes of former gayety can be found. The spring remains, but it is overgrown with bushes and weeds and is seldom approached, even by the negroes living in its vicinity. The river, too, has filled up at this point, and where once was navigable water is now but a marsh, covered thickly over with a luxuriant growth of marsh grass and rushes.

The arrangement of the Custis house was as excellent as the regulations that ruled the life of its owner. A broad hallway runs through the centre of it, and upon this opened the rooms on either side. To the right, as you enter the building, was the large dinning-room, with the butler's pantry in the rear. Across the hall were two large rooms used as parlors and sitting-rooms, and at the end of that wing of the building was Mr. Custis' library and study. A long, low wing that extends for forty or fifty feet to the right of the mansion was occupied by Mrs. Custis and her daughter. There they had their private sitting-rooms, their sewing-rooms and other apartments that make a home pleasant and comfortable to women. The sleeping apartments were all on the upper floors and they were large rooms, well lighted and ventilated by the large and numerous windows. The kitchen and quarters for the house servants were detached from the house, and were located in the two brick and stuccoed buildings, then, as now, at the end of the dwelling.

But the feature of Mr. Custis' house, in which he took great pride, himself and which never failed to impress the visitor, was the collection of relics, both of Washington, and the ancestors of the Custis family, who preceded him. Of these relics, the portraits he possessed were first in the matter of interest. They represented better than anything else could the men and women of the past and gave a clearer idea of their appearance than could have been obtained without their aid.

One of the finest of these portraits was that of Col. Daniel Parke, painted by Sir Godfrey Kneller. It represented the gallant Colonel in a very rich court dress, and showed the medallion portrait of Queen Anne, which had been presented to Col. Parke by that gracious sovereign, on the occasion that he brought her information of Marlborough's victory at Blenheim. There was also a portrait of an old reformer, painted by Vandyke, which was very valuable. Near these two hung portraits of John Custis, who married Col. Parke's daughter, and of his son, John Parke Custis, the first husband of Mrs. Washington. The latter was painted by Woolloston, and beside it was an early portrait of Mrs. Washington, then Mrs. Custis, painted by the same artist. Mr. Custis possessed two other portraits of Mrs. Washington, taken from life, one an exquisitely wrought miniature, by Robertson, painted in New York in 1791, and the other a profile in colored crayons by Sharpless.

But it was to the portraits of Washington himself that Mr. Custis attached the most value. One of these, painted by Charles Wilson Peale in 1772, represented Washington as he appeared at forty years of age. He was dressed in the costume of a Virginia colonel of that day. Another portrait, by Sharpless, showing Washington's profile, was considered the best likeness of the patriot ever executed. There was also in the collection a painting on copper showing the profiles of Washington and Lafayette side by side, in imitation of a medallion. This was painted by the Marchioness de Brienne, and presented by her to Washington in 1789. There were also fine portraits of Nellie Custis, George Washington Lafayette, and of others, rendered famous by their association with Washington.

Among the relics of Washington which Mr. Custis cherished were a sideboard, tea-table, and china punch-bowl, the latter a gift to Washington from the French naval officers; the large lantern that had illuminated the hallway at Mount Vernon; Washington's silver tea set, including a massive tray or salver; rich porcelain vases, mahogany chairs, several pieces of an elegant set of china, appropriately painted, and which were presented to Washington by the Society of the Cincinnati; part of another set presented to Mrs. Washington by the French officers; silver wine coolers and coasters; a harpsichord, presented to Nellie Custis by Washington before her marriage to Lawrence Lewis; massive silver candlesticks, with silver snuffers and extinguishers attached; a mural candelabra; the bed on which Washington died; his war tent, and the portmanteau in which it was carried, and other matters of minor interest.

There was also Washington's camp-chest, and a small iron chest, in which Mrs. Washington had kept certificates for 30,000 pounds sterling, a part of the fortune she brought Washington when she married him.

Not the least interesting of the pictures at Arlington were the battle scenes painted by Mr. Custis himself. These were principally painted on the walls of the rooms, and, while very poor works of art, they represented with some accuracy the figures and costumes of Washington and others as they appeared during the stirring scenes of the Revolution. There were five of these war scenes, and they represented, as near as Mr. Custis could make them, the battles of Monmouth, Trenton, Princeton, and Germantown; the surrender at Yorktown, and the surrender of the British colors at the same place. In each of these Washington is the central figure.

Painting these scenes was one of the pleasant diversions of Mr. Custis' later years, and after he had finished the pictures mentioned he painted a number of hunting scenes. A remnant of one of these is still to be seen in the frieze about the vestibule at the rear entrance to the Arlington mansion.

When the war broke out and the occupation of Arlington by Federal troops succeeded close upon the departure of Gen. and Mrs. Lee for the Confederate capital, all Mr. Custis' art and other treasures were scattered in every direction.

Some of the Washington relics had been deposited by Mr. Custis, previous to his death, with the Government, and now form the principal part of the Washington collection in the National Museum. When they first came into the possession of the Government they were placed on exhibition in the museum of the Patent Office, where they remained until the establishment of the National Museum, in 1876.

A number of the paintings were taken away from Arlington by Gen. and Mrs. Lee, and are still in the possession of the Lee family.

A great many of the relics, however, were seized upon by the vandals who followed and accompanied the Union forces. Cups that had been used by Washington himself were hawked about the streets of the National Capital by peddlers. Negroes enjoying newly-acquired liberty offered for sale articles the value of which would have purchased the seller at any time before the war, while soldiers with an appreciation of the character of the treasures they found upon the estate either purchased or purloined them as presents for wives and sweethearts in the distant northern States. Some of these scattered relics have since been collected, and are now either in the National Museum or at Mount Vernon. The Government has for years endeavored to secure every memorial of Washington that it can, and a number of the articles stolen or otherwise obtained from the Arlington house have since the war been purchased by those in charge of the National Museum. To many of these relics so acquired the heirs of Gen. R. E. Lee have laid claim, and the question of ownership is now pending in the civil courts.

The articles in dispute, now in the possession of the Government, are not on exhibition, but are carefully stowed away in boxes, awaiting the courts' decision.

While Mr. Custis' literary efforts have been mentioned frequently in the preceding pages, they really amounted to little of value, except for the recollections of Washington and the conversations with Lafayette, which are almost invaluable to the student of the early history of the country. His work was generally of the purposeless order, and very little of it has been preserved. He wrote poems and dramas for his own amusement and for the gratification of his friends.

The following extract from a letter addressed to his wife, then on a visit to some of her relatives, in 1833, may give an idea of the manner in which Mr. Custis performed his literary feats:

"I have made a great mental effort lately, but I am sure you and the Bishop will think my energies might have been better employed.

"I had promised the poor rogues of actors a play for the 12th of September, the anniversary of the battle of North Point, but finding myself not in the vein, I wrote to them to defer it. On Monday the 9th the manager came on from Baltimore, and entreated me to prepare something for the 12th, as it would put six or seven hundred dollars in his pocket. On Monday not a line was finished. At five o'clock I commenced and wrote until twelve; rose the next morning at five and by seven sent off by the stages a two-act piece, with two songs and a finale, called North Point; or,

Baltimore Defended, the whole completed in nine hours. It is to be played to-night. To-morrow I shall hear of its success. The principal character is called Marietta. She runs away from her father disguised as a rifle boy, etc., etc."

This letter not only shows the style of Mr. Custis' efforts, but gives an amusing insight into the condition of the American drama at that time. A theatrical manager accepts a play written in nine hours and produces it two days after it is completed, and Mr. Custis, the author, waits complacently at Arlington for the Baltimore papers, which he is sure will contain an account of the unqualified success of his highly-wrought imaginings.

A definite idea of Mr. Custis' home-life could hardly be obtained without some knowledge of the men and women who were his guests at Arlington. They were the descendants from the patriots of the Revolution, the representatives of the best families of Virginia, and distinguished men, both old and young, from the National Capital. Mrs. Lewis, Custis' sister, before and after the death of her husband, was as much at Arlington as at her own home. The Masons, from their fine old mansion on what was then Mason's Island, but now is Analostan Island, and the more distinguished family of old Col. Mason, of Gunston, near Mt. Vernon, were constant visitors. The Randolphs, the Fitzhughs, and scores of other well-known people in Virginia also found and appreciated the hearty welcome of the simple old man at Arlington. Henry Clay, Daniel Webster, and other statesmen were frequent guests, and amidst the throng, forming one of the conspicuous figures, was the then dashing and highly regarded young officer, Lieut. Robert E. Lee, of the United States Army.

CHAPTER IV.

LEE AT ARLINGTON—GENEALOGY AND EARLY CAREER—HIS SERVICE IN THE MEXICAN WAR.

The advent of Robert E. Lee at Arlington marks the beginning of an important epoch in the history of the famous estate. From this time on the fine old mansion is as inseparably connected with recollections of the hero of the Confederacy as it is with those concerning Custis himself, and its transfer at the old man's death from the descendants of Martha Washington to those of Light Horse Harry Lee, of the Revolution, was but an advance in the direction of its high destiny.

It was not, however, the beauty of Arlington, or its associations, that drew Lieut. Lee to the estate when he became a visitor there. Nor did the relics of Washington or the genial and admirable qualities of Mr. Custis play any very important part in attracting the young officer. His visits were, in fact, due principally to the presence in Arlington House of a very beautiful young lady, Miss Mary Custis, Mr. Custis' only child. Lieut. Lee's attentions were well received by Miss Custis, and on June 30, 1831, they were married in the main drawing-room of the Arlington Mansion, the room in which visitors are now requested to register their names. The marriage ceremony was witnessed by a large circle of guests, and was performed by the Rev. William Meade, afterwards bishop of Virginia. An amusing incident occurred at the wedding which has frequently been related.

In the early evening, preceding the hour set for the wedding, while Rev. Mr. Meade was journeying towards Arlington, a heavy thunder-storm came up and thoroughly drenched the good clergyman. When he arrived at the house he found the guests all waiting for him, impatient for the ceremony to begin. It was, of course, impossible for Mr. Meade to think of marrying any one while the clothes he wore were soaked with water. To obviate the difficulty, Mr. Custis attempted to supply him with a suit of his own. Unluckily for the fit of these garments, Mr. Custis was short and stout, the clergyman was tall and thin, and his appearance, when finally arrayed in them, was extremely ridiculous. However, the ample folds of the surplice covered all defects of raiment, and the guests generally were unaware of the awkward predicament of the dignified divine.

The marriage of Lieut. Lee to the heiress of Arlington added to the gayety of life on the estate. It was in the days before marriage journeys were fashionable, and the newly-married couple settled down to housekeeping in the good old style. Lieut. Lee had his estate at Stratford, left him by his father, to which he would have taken his bride, but the young lady preferred remaining at Arlington, and as Mr. Custis desired that the young people remain with him, they took up their abode there and made it their home at Mr. Custis' request, until his death, when the property passed into the possession of Col. and Mrs. Lee.

The death of Mr. Custis occurred in 1857 and produced a marked sensation throughout the country. He was ill only a short time, but his disease was pulmonary pneumonia, and four days after he was compelled to take to his bed he expired. After a night of insensibility he roused himself, and, with that transient gleam of light that usually precedes dissolution, he embraced each member of his family and took leave of the old servant who attended him. He requested that his pastor be summoned, and when the clergyman arrived asked that those present join in a prayer for the dying. While the prayer was being offered he expired. The funeral of Mr. Custis took place at Arlington and was attended by a vast concourse of people, in which were men of distinction in every walk of life. The Mount Vernon Guards of Alexandria, the Association of Survivors of the War of 1812 of the District of Columbia, a delegation of the Jamestown Society, field and staff officers of the volunteer regiment, the Washington Light Infantry, and a delegation of the President's mounted troop, all travelled to Arlington to unite in the solemn testimonials of respect.

Mr. Custis' remains were interred in what was then a beautiful grave, a short distance from the mansion. They were laid beside those of his wife, whose death had occurred two years earlier, and over the two graves were erected monuments which still stand amidst the grave-stones that mark the resting-places of thousands of Federal soldiers, a link connecting the past age with the present. With the death of Mr. Custis all the vast estates he possessed passed to his daughter, Mrs. Lee, and Arlington became the homestead of the Lees.

It was not the intention of the writers to introduce into this volume any matter historical or otherwise that has no direct bearing upon the history of the estate or those who lived within its precincts, but a sketch of the life of Gen. R. E. Lee while he made his home at Arlington, together with some account of his distinguished ancestry, seems to be indispensable to the completeness of the work.

While no additional lustre can be thrown on the achievements of Gen. Lee by any reference to his ancestry, it is worthy of remark that the family from which he sprung has an honorable place in the chronicles of every epoch of English history from the Norman invasion, and in the annals of the American colonial period from the time the family first appeared in this country.

When William the Conqueror landed upon the shores of Britain and flung his armies of mailed knights against the opposing Saxons, Launcelot Lee was one of the party of nobles that formed his personal escort. On the field of Hastings he was one of the most distinguished of that band of invaders and performed such signal service for his king that he was rewarded with large estates in Essex. He became the founder of the family that bears his name.

When the lion-hearted but erratic Richard, more than a century later, in 1192, conducted the Third Crusade into the Holy Land, Lionel Lee was one of the many nobles that accompanied him. He rode at the head of a company of "gentlemen cavaliers," and displayed such gallantry and courage at the siege of Acre that he was made Earl of Litchfield, while another estate, afterwards called "Ditchley," was also bestowed upon him. In the Horse Armory of the Tower of London may still be seen the armor worn by Lionel Lee in this crusade.

Two of the family were Knights-Companions of the Garter, and their banners, surmounted by the Lee arms, were placed in St. George's Chapel, at Windsor Castle.

Sir Henry Lee was Knight of the Garter in the reign of Queen Elizabeth. The Earldom of Litchfield passed to the fifth baronet of his line in 1674.

From Richard Lee, a younger son of the house of Litchfield, the line of descent of Gen. Lee can be directly traced. This Richard Lee in 1641, during the reign of Charles I., came to America as colonial secretary under the governorship of Sir William Berkeley. He was possessed of all those qualities which had made his family a line of commanders and soon obtained such influence over the colonists that Governor Berkeley, with his assistance, was able to keep Virginia firm in allegiance to the king and the loyalist party. When the second Charles was still in exile and without a kingdom, he was invited to come to Virginia and rule over his loving and devoted subjects in that colony. By reason of this act Virginia was styled, in a treaty made with the Commonwealth forces, an "Independent Dominion," this being the origin of the sobriquet it has since borne, "the Old Dominion." The king showed his gratitude for the loyalty exhibited by the colony by ordering the arms of Virginia to be added to those of England, France, Ireland, and Scotland, with the motto, "*En dat Virginia quintam.*"

It will thus be seen that the Lees were at once and at this early period of history fully identified with the country of their adoption.

The county of Westmoreland, with its diversity of hill and dale, its mild climate, fertile soil, and attractive scenery, at an early period won the attention of the Washingtons, Fairfaxes, Lees, and other distinguished families, and they naturally established their homes in this attractive situation. Here they evinced many of the traits, characteristics, and customs of English society.

Frequently they made the country ring with the merry sound of the horn and the hound as they swept through field and wood in pursuit of the wily fox or the bounding stag. In the life and habits of those people, and others of like descent and customs, was formed the germ of that martial spirit which characterizes what is called the "chivalry of Virginia." Gen. Lee himself as boy followed the chase for hours, not infrequently on foot, over hill and valley, laying the foundation of that vigor and robustness that enabled him so easily to overcome the fatigues and endure the hardships of war.

Richard Lee, second son of the Richard above named, was born in Virginia in 1646, and after being educated in law in England returned to Virginia and took an active part in colonial legislation. His fourth son, Thomas Lee, was the first of the family to locate in Westmoreland county. He attained high distinction in America and England, and grew to be one of the most prominent men in the early history of Virginia, in which province he became successively president of the council and governor of the colony, being the first native-born American who held the latter office under the British Crown. In colonial history he is known as "President Lee."

The fine mansion of Stratford, in Westmoreland county, the birthplace of Robert E. Lee, two signers of the Declaration of Independence, and several other famous members of the family, was built for Thomas Lee by the East India Company, aided by an ample donation from the privy purse of Queen Caroline, his former residence having been burned. This structure, which is still standing, was built of bricks imported from England, in the substantial manner common in those days, the walls of the first story being two feet and a half thick, those of the second story two feet. It was even more spacious than the neighboring colonial mansions, containing in all nearly a hundred rooms.

Thomas Lee died in 1756, leaving eight children—six sons and two daughters. Several of his sons occupied prominent places in the colonial history of America, while three of them, Richard Henry, Francis Lightfoot, and Arthur Lee, deserve particular mention from their connection with the American revolution.

Richard Henry Lee was a member of the House of Burgesses of Virginia, and afterward became a distinguished member of the Continental Congress. He is best known as one of the great orators of that period, and to him is due that stirring resolution of the 10th of June, 1776, which proclaimed to the world that America was full grown and ready to take its allotted place in the family of nations—the resolution "that these United Colonies are, and of right ought to be, free and independent States; that they are absolved from all allegiance to the British Crown, and that all political connection between them and Great Britain is, and ought to be, totally absolved."

Francis Lightfoot Lee was also a member of the Continental Congress and was one of the signers of the Declaration of Independence; while Arthur Lee was entrusted in the all-important foreign mission on behalf of the new republic.

Robert E. Lee is descended directly from Richard Lee of the second generation of the family in America, and the father of Thomas Lee just described. The descent is traced from Henry, the fifth son of Richard, and the direct ancestor of the subject of this story.

Henry Lee occupied no prominent place in colonial history, his life being that of a student, though, like his brother, he occupied a place in the early councils of the colony. He married a Miss Bland and had three children.

The second son, Henry, became a member of the House of Burgesses and took an active part in the exciting political events of the time. He was married in 1753 to Lucy Grymes, a descendant of General Thomas Grymes, of Cromwell's army. He left a large family, six sons and five daughters. The eldest son, who bore the name of his father, was born in 1756, near Dumfries on the Potomac, and was distinguished for the character of his services in the Revolutionary war, being best known by the dashing title he earned early in the war, "Light Horse Harry" Lee.

He was the father of Robert E. Lee.

At an early age this third Henry Lee in direct descent was sent to Princeton College, where he distinguished himself as a law student. On completing his studies here he was about starting for England when the outbreak of hostilities caused him to change his plans. He was then nineteen years of age. He abandoned his intention of going to England, and quickly raising a company of cavalry he joined Washington soon after the battle of Lexington. His energy and ability soon earned him a high reputation, and he was speedily promoted to the rank of lieutenant-colonel and assigned the command of an independent corps composed of infantry and cavalry, and known as "Lee's Legion." His services were conspicuous during the war, and at the close of the Revolution none had acquired a more permanent and deserved reputation than "Light Horse Harry" Lee. About the year 1781 he was married to his cousin Matilda, daughter of Philip Ludwell Lee, by which marriage the homestead at Stratford came into his possession.

He was elected to Congress soon after the close of the war and afterwards became Governor of Virginia, to which office he was three times elected.

During the year 1790 he lost his wife, who had borne him four children. These had all died except the eldest, Henry. After several years of retirement from public life he married Mrs. Anne Hill Carter, daughter of Charles Carter, of Shirley, by whom he had five children, Charles Carter Lee, of Powhattan; Sidney Smith Lee, a commander in the United States Navy in 1860, and afterward in Confederate States Navy; and Robert E. Lee. The two daughters were Anne and Mildred.

Robert Lee was born in the same room at Stratford in which were born Richard, Henry, and Francis Lightfoot Lee.

Henry Lee in 1798 returned to public life and became a member of the General Assembly, and afterwards was re-elected to Congress.

On the death of Washington he prepared the eulogy by direction of Congress, in which occur the memorable words which have become indissolubly attached to the name of the hero of the Revolution: "First in war, first in peace, first in the hearts of his countrymen."

In 1811 he removed to Alexandria for the purpose of educating his children, and while here was offered and accepted a major-general's commission during the second war with England. At the close of the year 1817, declining health induced him to visit the West Indies, but obtaining no relief from the tropical climate he determined to return to his native home. Rapidly failing health on his return voyage caused him to direct his course to the coast of Georgia, where, at the home of the daughter of his old comrade, Gen. Greene, on Cumberland Island, he died after a short illness.

His neglected grave is but a short distance from the now dismantled mansion, in a wildly overgrown garden of magnolias and sub-tropical shrubbery.

Gen. Lee, as before stated, was born January 19, 1807, in the old manor-house at Stratford which came into the possession of his father through his marriage with his cousin, a member of the other branch of the Lees. The old mansion is best described in the language of Gen. R. E. Lee himself:

"The approach to the house is on the south, along the side of a lawn, several hundred acres in extent, adorned with cedars, oaks, and forest poplars. On ascending a hill not far from the gate the traveller comes in full view of the mansion, when the road turns to the right and leads straight to a grove of sugar maples, around which it sweeps to the house. The edifice is built in the form of an H and of bricks brought from England. The cross furnishes a saloon of thirty feet cube, and in the centre of each wing rises a cluster of four chimneys which form the columns of two pavilions, connected by a balustrade. The owner, who, before the Revolution, was a member of the King's Council, lived here in great state, and kept a band of musicians, to whose airs his daughters, Matilda and Flora, with their companions, danced in the saloon or promenaded on the house-top."

Here young Lee lived until 1811, when his father removed to Alexandria to give his children the benefit of the educational advantages offered by that town, then a thriving and prosperous municipality. The family lived on Cameron street, near the old Christ church, then on Orinoco street, and afterwards in the house known as the parsonage. The young lad's character was moulded by his mother, under whose sole influence he came during his boyhood. His father was absent for long periods on duty as major-general in the American army, and in the later years of his life engaged in a despairing search after the spirit of health that had forsaken him. Robert in these years became a familiar figure in the streets of the old Virginia town, where he formed many lifelong friendships. He was devoted to his invalid mother, and bestowed upon her the most faithful care and attention and made her welfare the chief object of his thoughts. He was a thoughtful, earnest youth and spent his hours out of school at his mother's side.

When he entered school at Alexandria he had as his first teacher an Irish gentleman, William B. Leary, who, even before his famous pupil had become in any way distinguished, held him up to the boys that came after him as a model student. His early education was obtained from Mr. Leary, under whose tuition he remained until it was decided that he should go to West Point.

He then took a preparatory course under Mr. Benjamin Hallowell, a famous teacher of mathematics in Alexandria. In 1825, when he was eighteen years of age, he entered the Military Academy at West Point, where he remained four years, graduating in 1829 at the head of his class. At the time of Lee's marriage to Miss Custis he had been an officer of the United States Army for two years. The high honors he had secured as a student at the Military Academy caused his assignment to the engineer corps, then, as now, the highest branch of the service, and his first military duty was in connection with that corps. He was first ordered to Cockspur Island, near Savannah, but after his marriage was sent to Old Point, where he remained until 1835. In that year he was appointed assistant astronomer to mark out the boundary line between Ohio and Michigan, and as a result of this service he was promoted to the rank of captain. Capt. Lee was stationed for the next two years in Washington, as assistant to Chief Engineer Gratiot. During this time he lived at Arlington and might have been seen morning and evening of each pleasant day riding along Pennsylvania avenue, on his way between his Virginia home and the War Department. While in Washington he numbered among his associates Lieuts. J. E. Johnston and M. C. Meigs, one of whom was in later years his most trusted confidant, the other his most implacable enemy. At that time, however, they were all good friends, and in 1837, when Capt. Lee was ordered to take charge of the engineering operations in the Mississippi, Lieut. Meigs went along as his assistant. The work which was entrusted to Capt. Lee at this time was of a very important character and its completion was not only regarded as an important engineering achievement, but rendered possible the present city of St. Louis. St. Louis was at the time threatened with a serious disaster from the deflection of the main current of the Mississippi to the Illinois side and the danger of its cutting a new channel through the bottom lands. Sand bars were forming along the city's entire river front and threatened to interfere with, if not to ruin altogether, its harbor.

In addition to remedying this, Capt. Lee was instructed to make surveys and plans for improving the river where the Des Moines river enters it from the west, and about the mouth of the Rock river, which enters from the east. At both these points the river flowed over ledges of rock, with a narrow and tortuous channel, and during the season of low water all steamboats were obliged to discharge at least a part of their cargoes in order to get through. After working with his party for several months Capt. Lee made up his report and it was submitted to Congress by the Secretary of War. He recommended the improvement of the two rapids by the straightening and widening of the channels and by blasting and moving the rocks that obstructed navigation. In regard to St. Louis, he recommended the proper course of the dykes to deflect the currents and to close at low water the eastern or Illinois channel by connecting Bloody Island with the eastern shore. Upon these recommendations Congress continued for a number of years to make the necessary appropriations for the execution of the work, and a portion of it was accomplished under Capt. Lee's supervision. A good description of Gen. Lee, as he impressed others at this time, was written by Gen. Meigs. Gen. Meigs wrote of him:

"He was a man then in the vigor of youthful strength, with a noble and commanding presence, and an admirable, graceful, and athletic figure. He was one with whom nobody ever wished or ventured to take a liberty, though kind and generous to his subordinates, admired by all women and respected by all men. He was the model of a soldier and the beau ideal of a Christian man."

Capt. Lee continued to render valuable services to his government as an engineer, a portion of the time at Fort Hamilton, in New York harbor, and at other points, until the breaking out of hostilities between the United States and Mexico. During these years, so well employed, he was for a time one of the board of visitors to the Military Academy at West Point, and did much to improve the course of training at that institution.

With every branch of work to which he had been assigned, with every difficult operation he had undertaken, Capt. Lee proved himself an officer of remarkable ability, unswerving in his devotion to duty, and he was rapidly pressing forward to the very foremost rank of distinction and honor in military circles.

The commencement of the Mexican war opened a wider field for the exercise of his abilities as a military engineer and offered his first opportunity for that practical education in the art of war which was afterward to bear such abundant fruit. No officer who participated in the campaign in Mexico achieved more distinction or rendered more valuable service than did Capt. Lee. He was assigned to Gen. Wool's command at the opening of the war and remained with it until after the battle of Buena Vista, in which Gen. Taylor with a force of 5,000 men put to rout Santa Anna's force of 20,000 men, when, at the request of Gen. Scott, Lee joined his army in the neighborhood of Tampico.

On the 9th of March, 1847, Gen. Scott landed his army of 12,000 men a short distance south of Vera Cruz, and laid siege to the city. It was strongly fortified by walls, and defended by a powerful fortress, the castle of San Juan de Ulloa, garrisoned by 5,000 men and containing 400 heavy guns. The establishment of batteries and the arrangement of all the other engineering details of the siege were directed by Capt. Lee, and so well was his work performed that on the 22d it had been completed, and on the 29th the city surrendered. Having gained by the capture of Vera Cruz a secure base of operations, Gen. Scott advanced on the city of Mexico. Santa Anna with a strong force took up a position on the National Road at Cerro Gordo, where he so strongly entrenched himself that further advance was impossible, while battle in so disadvantageous a position would have been sure to result disastrously for the American forces. Capt. Lee was therefore sent out to make reconnoissances, and at the end of the third day a passage for light batteries was accomplished around Santa Anna's entire army without alarming it. This rendered possible the turning of the extreme left of the enemy's line of defence, and capturing his entire army. A large force was sent along the route, thus made passable by Capt. Lee, and it had gained a position from which it was able to storm the heights of Cerro Gordo, and rout the entire Mexican army before it was discovered. For his services on this occasion and also at Vera Cruz, Capt. Lee was highly praised in the reports of the commander-in-chief. In the engagement at San Augustin, and Contreras which followed, Capt. Lee again distinguished himself by his courage and sagacity.

The Mexicans occupied a very strong position, while the Americans were obliged to advance over a region of country so broken that horses could hardly keep a foothold. Pillow's and Twiggs' divisions were sent forward and with them went Capt. Lee. They started from San Augustin, where Gen. Scott had his headquarters, and by night they had fought their way over the broken ground to Contreras. There a council of war was held, which was counselled by Capt. Lee, and the plan of future operations decided upon at his suggestion. When the council closed, Capt. Lee announced his intention of returning to San Augustin to report the conclusions of the meeting to Gen. Scott. A more hazardous undertaking than this could hardly have been conceived of. It was night and the darkness was intensified by a severe rain-storm, which was pouring its torrents upon the heroic band of American soldiers. The country lying between Contreras and San Augustin was almost impassable in the daytime, while, to add to the danger, the American forces were almost completely hemmed in by Mexican troops. Notwithstanding these difficulties, however, Capt. Lee persisted in his determination, and without a companion or a light made the journey so fraught with danger, and arrived in safety at Gen. Scott's camp. His achievement called forth from Gen. Scott the highest commendation, and the whole American army applauded the gallant conduct of the daring officer.

As a result of Capt. Lee's prompt report, Gen. Scott advanced his entire army under Capt. Lee's guidance, and at daylight an attack upon the enemy's strongholds was made. In the battle Lee again distinguished himself, and so well planned was the attack he had rendered possible, that in just seventeen minutes the Mexicans were driven from their works and were in full retreat.

In all the subsequent events of the war Lee played a prominent part, gradually rising in the esteem of his commanders, of his brother officers, and in his rank in the service. One promotion followed another in rapid succession, and after the brilliant charge at Chapultepec, in which he was severely wounded, he received the rank of brevet colonel. He was Gen. Scott's favorite officer, and so well had he earned the favor shown him, that his fellow-soldiers applauded their commander for his recognition of Lee's brilliant services.

When peace between the United States and Mexico had been established by the conclusion of the treaty negotiations, Col. Lee returned home with the victorious army and was again assigned to duty in the corps of engineers. He was engaged in the construction of fortifications at Sallers Point, near Baltimore, at Hampton Roads, and in New York harbor until 1852, when he was appointed superintendent of the U. S. Military Academy at

West Point. He occupied this position until 1855, when he was promoted to a command in the cavalry branch of the service, and, as colonel of the Second cavalry, was placed in charge of the department of Texas. At this time Texas and the country adjoining was overrun by bands of hostile Indians, who let no opportunity escape to massacre and rob the settlers whenever the latter ventured beyond the protecting arm of the military. To keep these maurauders in subjection and to protect the settlers, was the duty which now devolved upon Gen. Lee and his small command. Bloody engagements were frequent between the troops and the savages, and as hard a campaign of frontier warfare as any in the history of the country was carried on.

In these campaigns he was engaged until within a short time of the breaking out of the Civil war. It is a matter worthy of note that while in his earlier career Col. Lee had been intimately associated with such officers as Meigs, Beauregard, McClellan, and others, who afterwards achieved great distinction, in his Indian wars he had as officers of his command Johnson, Hardee, Thomas, Van Dorn, Hood, Fitz Lee, Stoneman, Kirby Smith, and Fields, all of whom became general officers in either the Confederate or Federal service during the Civil war. While at Camp Cooper, Texas, in 1857, Col. Lee received notice by telegraph of the death of his wife's father, G. W. P. Custis, and at once hastened to Arlington. He returned to Texas, however, and remained there until the state of excitement prevailing throughout the country rendered, in the opinion of the War Department, his presence at the National Capital necessary.

Although Col. Lee had been very actively engaged in the service of his country, while the discordant elements throughout the North and South were fomenting the difficulties surrounding the slave question until the land was overcast with the shadows of threatening clouds of civil war, he had, notwithstanding, found time to watch with ever-increasing anxiety the formation of the breach between the sections.

Though opposed to the institution of slavery, which he regarded as a moral and political evil, he was of the unalterable opinion that the matter was one that under the Constitution the States had the right to regulate for themselves, and he denied absolutely the right of the non-holding slave States to interfere. He believed the emancipation of the negroes would sooner result from the mild and melting influences of Christianity than from the storm and tempest of fiery controversy. He was too much of a patriot to believe that the country could possibly be disrupted over the question, but he saw with feelings of the gravest apprehension that it was, as he expressed it, rushing rapidly towards the verge of anarchy or civil war.

Having been recalled to Washington, Lee took up his residence at Arlington, and was there when the John Brown raid on Harper's Ferry occurred. He was at once summoned to Washington by the Secretary of War and directed to take command of a battalion of marines and proceed to the scene of the outbreak.

When he arrived at Harper's Ferry he found Brown and his followers located in the Government building closely besieged by the militia troops that had assembled there. Col. Lee stationed his troops around the building and sent Lieut. J. E. B. Stuart with a flag of truce to demand the surrender of the insurgents.

On their refusal to capitulate Col. Lee charged the building with his men, broke open the door, and released the citizens who had been imprisoned as hostages by Brown, before any of them could be injured. In the fight all the insurgents but Brown and three others were killed, while Lee's small command also suffered a considerable loss. But for the protection afforded Brown by Col. Lee, he would in all probability have been lynched by the indignant citizens of Harper's Ferry. Lee, however, held him as a prisoner, and as such turned him over to the civil authorities.

After this service Col. Lee returned to Texas, where for the next year he watched with growing uneasiness the discord between the North and South.

Events now crowded upon each other with such rapidity that there could no longer be any doubt that civil war was to be the final result and that the conflict was irrepressible and inevitable. The election of Mr. Lincoln in 1860 spread consternation throughout the South, and a similar degree of excitement prevailed in the North when the delegates from the Southern States withdrew in a body from the Congress of the United States.

Then followed the secession of South Carolina, and in February of 1861 the seven cotton States united themselves into an independent republic, and demanded the surrender of Fort Sumter, at Montgomery, Alabama. Following this, and thrilling the country with the intelligence that civil war, cruel and relentless, was on at last, came the news of Sumter's bombardment and surrender. The fortress fell beneath the fearful fire of shot and shell from the Confederate batteries on April 13, and on April 15 President Lincoln issued a proclamation calling for 75,000 volunteers. Just two days later the convention of Virginia passed the ordinance of secession, and the entire country was involved in the greatest civil strife the world has ever seen. In all this preparation for war, Col. Lee was recalled from Texas, and on March 1, 1861, he arrived in Washington in response to an order issued by the War Department.

It had been Col. Lee's intention at this time, in case Virginia were not involved in the struggle for State's rights, to retire to his home at Arlington, and there sheathe his sword forever, rather than take part in so unnatural a war as that between the States of so great a union. The secession of Virginia cast the die for him, however, and without hesitation he joined his fortunes with those of the Southern Confederacy.

His final decision was not reached without severe mental trouble nor without efforts on the part of the Government to preserve his highly valued services to the Federal army. He was offered positions of the highest importance and honor, and was indirectly promised the position of Commander-in-chief of the Union forces. This offer was made him by Francis Preston Blair, the father of Montgomery Blair, then Postmaster-General. Mr. Blair, during their interview, informed Col. Lee that he had been sent by President Lincoln and he inquired whether any inducement would prevail upon Lee to take command of the Union army. Lee replied that to lift his hand against his native State would be impossible.

Immediately after this interview Col. Lee went to the office of Gen. Scott, to whom he related what had transpired. Then he returned to Arlington, and after two days spent in a severe mental struggle to determine on which side his duty lay, he concluded to resign his commission in the army. His letter of resignation was written at Arlington, on Saturday, April 20, and is as follows:

ARLINGTON, VA., *April* 20, 1861.

GENERAL: Since my interview with you on the 18th inst. I have felt that I ought not longer to retain my commission in the army. I therefore tender my resignation, which I request you will recommend for acceptance. It would have been presented at once but for the struggle it has cost me to separate myself from a service to which I have devoted all the best years of my life and all the ability I possessed. During the whole of that time—more than a quarter of a century—I have experienced nothing but kindness from my superiors and a most cordial friendship from my comrades. To no one, General, have I been as much indebted as to yourself for uniform kindness and consideration, and it has always been my ardent desire to merit your approbation. I shall carry to the grave the most grateful recollections of your consideration, and your name and fame will be always dear to me. Save in the defence of my native State, I never desire again to draw my sword. Be pleased to accept my most earnest wishes for the continuance of your happiness and prosperity, and believe me most truly yours,

R. E. LEE.

This letter, though written on the 20th, was not sent to Gen. Scott until Monday, the 22d. On the same day Col. Lee, with Mrs. Lee and their children, left Arlington for Richmond, never to return. On the day following, Tuesday, the 23d of April, Lee accepted the position of Commander-in-chief of the forces of Virginia.

CHAPTER V.

SEIZURE AND OCCUPATION OF ARLINGTON BY FEDERAL FORCES—THE FIRST INTERMENT.

Three days after the Lee family left Arlington the first battalions of the great army of the North swept into the District of Columbia, and the first camp-fires were lighted among the oaks of Arlington.

The place was found just as it had been left. John McQuin, a faithful overseer of the family, remained in charge of the house and grounds, and every morning the great doors of the mansion were flung open in hospitable welcome, and at night closed and barred with the same scrupulous care that had attended this formal ceremony when the occupants of the house had retired to their rooms, in the uneventful days before the clarion trump of war had sounded the death of tranquillity and domesticity in Virginia.

When the armed troops swarmed up the Arlington hillsides they found the house open to them, the walks cleaned, the gardens cleared and trimmed, as though the master of the house were yet within to give them welcome. When they tramped into the echoing rooms they found none to receive them, and as they rummaged from cellar to garret the loved treasures of Washington were taken out and divided among the recruits, who knew not but that they were the possessions of Lee himself and so felt no compunctions upon carrying them off as trophies of war.

The mansion itself became the headquarters of the commanders of the troops quartered on the grounds, and soon long lines of tents forming company streets had sprung up all over the hillsides and out over the level plateau to the south. Drills by battalions and regiments were held daily and soon the place had seemingly lost its identity in the great transformation that had been wrought.

The ancient stately manse that had formerly known no harsher sounds than the strains of sweet music or the prattle of children in innocent frolic, now resounded with the clank of sabre and accoutrements and the heavy tread of cavalry-booted officers.

The quiet, gentle life the place had formerly known gave way to the abrupt roughness of a military camp. Mud-bespattered orderlies dashed through the quiet, shaded avenues, and the smooth, level lawns were trampled into clayey plains by bands of wandering recruits. All the boundaries, garden plats, and smooth reaches of green turf that in times of peace were preserved inviolate by a natural respect for order and beauty were swept away, and even the gradually descending terraces were broken down and became but ragged embankments.

The place was never again to bear the loved title and beautiful name of "home." From this time until the war was ended Arlington remained in the possession of the military and was destined to ultimately receive to its kindly bosom, in the lethean caress of death, many of the brave lads that had so cheerfully and with such high hopes and ambitions first spread their tents amid its forests.

Early in the war Washington became the hospital base for all the section of the country surrounding, and thousands of wounded soldiers from the neighboring battle-fields were carried there by train and boat, as well as the many unused to the hardships and privations of warfare, who sickened in camp and on the field. In 1864 there were fifty-six hospitals in Washington, from St. Elizabeth's Asylum just across the Eastern Branch of the Potomac to the tents at Arlington. Private dwellings, warehouses, churches, and schools were converted into hospitals, and throughout Washington the groans of thousands of wounded heroes floated on the misery-laden air. The intertwined serpents and the green stripes and chevrons were the insignia most familiar to Washingtonians, for the surgeon and his staff everywhere had precedence.

On the hills of Arlington the long canvas shelters hemmed in the mansion on every side. The house itself was early in the war occupied by the officers of Fort Whipple, a garrison located on the hills west of Arlington, and was later shared with officers of Fort McPherson, an earthwork thrown up by McClellan a short distance south of the mansion. The surgeon's staff of the hospital corps also established headquarters here.

The great oaks immediately surrounding the house were preserved from destruction, and, under their grateful shade, stretched away long lines of white tents, sheltering the suffering victims of the rebellion's battles. Soft, whispering breezes crept through the long cathedral-like aisles of oak and elm, touching with pitying caress alike the brow of the childish recruit and the aged veteran. Death dwelt amid these tents and daily reaped a greater harvest than is yielded in a great city in many months. To many he came as a white-winged messenger of love and pity, bringing blessed surcease from pain and torture almost unbearable. Army ambulances, converted into hearses by the simple expedient of painting them a sombre black, passed about the city at all hours of the day and night garnering the harvest of death. From the hospitals in the city and from those without the bodies of the dead were taken to the Soldiers' Home Cemetery, then the only military cemetery in Washington.

Early in the spring of 1864 the interments made here had exhausted every available inch of space. Over 8,000 soldiers who had died in the hospitals in and about Washington had been buried in the cemetery, and in May those in charge reported that but a few more bodies could be interred, and the cemetery would then of necessity have to be closed and the further issue of burial permits denied.

By this time the disposal of the bodies of those who died at Washington became a serious problem. Gen. M. C. Meigs, then Quartermaster-General of the United States Army, was a man of infinite resources; but taxed to the utmost by the constant demands made upon on all sides he had but little attention to bestow upon these seemingly minor questions. The proper and decent burial of all Union soldiers who died in service he recognized, however, as being of the greatest importance. Throughout the North there existed a belief, unfounded on facts, but strong among the masses, that the Union dead were carelessly and irreverently buried. This feeling engendered great bitterness among the very classes from which Gen. Meigs felt must come the bone and sinew of the Union Army. The effect of this growing feeling he did not attempt to underestimate, and the news coming at this time that there was no available ground in which to inter the bodies of those then dying in the near-by hospitals caused him to lay aside for a time his other pressing duties to devote his attention entirely to this engrossing problem. He had several conferences with Secretary of War Stanton, who requested him to take immediate steps to quell the feeling arising in the North, and to provide, at any cost, adequate burial facilities.

Late in the afternoon on the 13th of May, 1864, Gen. Meigs left his office in the old War Department building, and buried in deep thought walked over into the grounds surrounding the White House, intent only on thinking out solutions to some of the many problems with which he had to contend. With eyes bent on the ground and enwrapped in thought he was just passing the White House portico when he was hailed by a familiar voice.

"Step in here, Meigs, and take a drive with me," said the President, "you look tired and worn out; you need a rest."

Gen. Meigs looked up quickly and saw the honest rugged face of Lincoln, lit by a half smile, more serious than mirthful.

Two iron grays stood pawing, restlessly impatient, and the soft cushions of the victoria looked invitingly comfortable. The President threw open the low door and the Quartermaster-General entered the vehicle. A moment later the team clattered down the driveway and the carriage whirled rapidly away toward Georgetown.

The street over which they passed was not the smooth, asphalted thoroughfare of to-day, but a rough, uneven dirt road, sending up great clouds of dust in dry weather, and changing to one vast pool of mud throughout its entire length during the rainy season. Over this miserable roadway, fronted upon but by few houses in the long stretch from the White House to Georgetown, rolled the coach of the President. In a few minutes the town across the creek was reached, and the heavy vehicle rumbled over a very superior quality of cobble-paving, for Georgetown was far in advance of the Capital in some respects. Past century-old houses with whose histories the names of the nation's greatest men are linked; past the old Key mansion, where dwelt the poet who has given us our most stirring national hymn, and out upon the Aqueduct clattered the spirited team. The two silent men, absorbed in their own thoughts, had talked but little; but now as the beauty of the scene, spread out in prospect, burst upon them they lapsed into absolute silence. The restive pair, held down to a walk, drew frettingly upon check and rein, and tossed their proud heads and champed with impatience upon their bits.

Toward the east there rose no magic city, robed in imperial

beauty, unequalled in the wide world, such as now greets the sight. A few miserable scattered hovels; here and there unsightly masses of masonry, the beginnings of great results in architecture, as yet inchoate and undefined, and the one great achievement of genius and art, the huge white dome of the Capitol, alone gave faint promise of the magnificent development of later years.

Toward the south and west, however, they gazed upon the same scenes that are presented to-day. Above the bridge, wooded hills, rocky islets, and the Chain Bridge, a noted strategic point in the earlier days of the war. Off to the south the forested island home of Gen. Mason, the last of a long colonial line, whose direct ancestors were daily visitors at Mount Vernon, and among Washington's dearest friends. This old mansion, of little beauty but of great strength of masonry and thick beams, is intimately connected with the classically beautiful mansion-house at Arlington, for between Gen. Mason and Mr. Custis there existed the most cordial friendship, and the two estates were one in all but boundaries. Over the oak-crowned hills of Mason Island Mr. Custis hunted with gun and hound, and at Arlington Gen. Mason was ever an honored guest.

The old mansion of the Masons is now in ruins, and the family is remembered only by the name the island once bore in the long ago, before the more beautiful Indian name it now bears was bestowed upon it.

Past Mason Island then, now Analostan Island, the carriage whirled rapidly along toward the camp at Arlington. On every hand sentinels saluted with presented pieces, and groups of strolling soldiers of all branches of the army paused and gazed wonderingly at the two men in the carriage. Arrived at the mansion-house at Arlington, the President alighted and started out for a stroll among the tents and across the lower portion of the estate to Fort McPherson, whose grim embankments crowned by frowning cannon arose from the level plateau stretching away toward the south.

These drives into the surrounding country were of frequent occurrence with President Lincoln, who took this means of throwing aside for a brief period the burdens of his position. After a day of trouble and turmoil in the White House, beset on all sides by clamors for advice or assistance, keyed to the highest tension by news from the seat of war, and by a full knowledge of the vast responsibilities devolving upon him, he was able at the end of the day to relax the tension and recuperate for another day of great effort by dropping entirely his character of Chief Magistrate and becoming again the genial, hearty, unaffected citizen. Gen. Meigs, however, did not possess the power to apply in similar manner the principles of the conservation of energy, and the difference in the temperament of the two men was shown strikingly in this case. Gen. Meigs had no sooner alighted than he began to busy himself in the affairs under the charge of his office at Arlington. He was in a few minutes deeply engaged in a conference with the corps of surgeons in charge of the hospital tents, and was more strongly than ever convinced of the necessity for immediate action in regard to the proper sepulture of the army's dead. After an hour, however, nothing had been accomplished and, the President having returned, the two men prepared to drive back to the city.

As they stood on the terrace in front of the mansion, awaiting the arrival of the carriage, both men were struck with the glorious natural beauty of the panorama spread out before them. From the placid shimmering bosom of the Potomac they turned their gaze across the broad level basin in which the Capital City lies and absorbed the beauty of the distant Maryland hills, clad in a mantle of changing tints of red and gold, as the last rays of the setting sun touched tenderly the sturdy forests that clothed their sides.

While the soft eventide breathed only peace and tenderness, Gen. Meigs' thoughts were keyed to harsher feelings. He dwelt reminiscently upon the long months spent in brotherly companionship with the absent Lee, but with retrospection the present grew clearer and a hatred and aversion for his former chum grew in his heart. While Lee had espoused the cause of the Confederacy, he had enlisted heart and brain in the active service of the North, and as the weary years of the war lengthened and the end came not in sight, all soft impulses died out of him, and there came instead the implacable feeling of bitterest enmity against the South and Southerners. To him the word "rebel" was synonymous with all that was base and treacherous, and the act of renunciation had to him cancelled all the good and noble qualities his young manhood's chum had possessed. He was angered at the happiness Lee must have experienced amid the beautiful surroundings of Arlington, and in his mind a resolution at once took tangible form.

"Lee shall never return to Arlington," he said abruptly, turning to the President. "No matter what the issue of the war may be, the arch-rebel shall never again enjoy the possession of these estates."

The President smiled good humoredly at the feeling words of the Quartermaster-General, and would have made some reply had not the attention of the men at that moment been called to a sad procession that passed within a few feet of them. On common canvas stretchers, borne by members of a detailed squad, were the bodies of several unfortunates who had died in the hospital tents. They were being carried to the lower part of the grounds to await the coming of the burial squad to convey them to the already overcrowded Soldiers' Home Cemetery. Stopping the sergeant in command of the squad, Gen. Meigs asked, "How many men are there awaiting burial here?" "With these, a dozen, sir," answered the sergeant; "no bodies have been taken away during the week."

"Set down the stretchers," commanded the Quartermaster-General, and then, turning to a commissioned officer standing near, he said: "Captain, order out a burial squad and see that all the bodies at Arlington are buried on the place at once." Then walking a few paces away he pointed out the slight terrace bordering the garden of the mansion, "Bury them there," he said.

The officer saluted and disappeared. The carriage of the President, which had drawn up a few minutes before, was standing ready, and President Lincoln and Gen. Meigs entered and were driven rapidly back to Washington.

A few minutes later a squad, in charge of a corporal, came quickly up the broad driveway in front of the mansion, with picks and shovels, and, stopping at the place indicated by Gen. Meigs, began at once the work of preparing the shallow receptacles that were to contain the remains of their dead fellows. Places for twelve graves were marked out about a dozen yards south of the house, and soon the yellow mounds of moist earth began to rise at the sides of the narrow pits.

In half an hour the labor was completed, and as the last of the clay-soiled workers emerged from the grave he had made and joined his comrades, a sombre black ambulance doing duty as a hearse and bearing within its gloomy interior the bodies of those who had died at Arlington drove slowly up the driveway. The bodies were in black pine coffins, and as the hearse halted they were quickly drawn forth and placed beside the graves that were to contain them.

The sun that but a short time before had blazed out behind the western hills and had massed the low hanging clouds into vast banks of glowing crimson, seen in brilliant glory through the black broad oaks of Arlington, was now low out of sight, and the early evening came on with the many noises of night, and the cool, steely blue of the nocturnal heaven had killed out the warm refulgent glow of the dying day. Darkness was coming on quickly, and down in the deep woods to the north the great flocks of crows had settled into quietness and harmony, announcing their presence only by an occasional discordant cawing. From the mansion came the chaplain, an elderly ecclesiast who, with more feeling than was common, read a burial service over the twelve bodies lying before him. The bodies were then quickly placed in the rude graves and the heavy lumps of clay thumped upon the lids with a dull monotonous regularity until there remained only twelve ghastly yellow mounds standing out sharply from the green lawn. The members of the squad shouldered their implements and were a few seconds later swallowed up in the grim forbidding forest that now loomed out in black massiveness about the mansion.

The first interment of Union dead had been made at Arlington.

CHAPTER VI.

ESTABLISHMENT OF THE NATIONAL CEMETERY—BODIES OF SOLDIERS COLLECTED ON THE BATTLE-FIELDS AND BURIED AT ARLINGTON.

In this manner, on the 13th of May, 1864, the national cemetery at Arlington was established. Gen. Meigs, by his decisive action, not only provided for the proper sepulture of the dead heroes of the Federal cause, but at the same time carried into effect his resolution to tear from the possession of the Confederate leader the beautiful estate that had been his home.

He knew that the united sentiment of the great North would never permit the desecration of the graves by the disinterment of the Union dead, and for this reason he ordered the first burials to be made around the edge of the garden near the house, in order to prevent any section of the grounds from being set aside for cemeterial purposes after the war, and, being thus cut off from the house and surrounding acres, to allow the latter to again be occupied by the Lee family or any of its members. It is an ill wind, however, that blows no good to any one, and Gen. Meigs by this bit of retributive malice secured to his country a monument to the martyrs who died "in the blue" that will endure when tablets of brass and shafts of granite shall have mouldered into dust. The everlasting hills, the groves of oak and elm will stand for centuries, nature's vast memorial cathedral, amid whose leafy aisles the errant wind shall murmur eternally a sad requiem, or in fiercer blast a jubilant pæan of martial glory.

The most striking fact in connection with the first burial at Arlington was that the first man interred was a rebel prisoner, L. Reinhardt, of the 23rd North Carolina regiment, who was taken captive in one of the battles about Washington and who died of his wounds in one of the Arlington hospital wards. His was the grave nearest the house and the first over which the few words of the brief burial service were read. His interment was registered as the first in a cemetery where now 16,000 bodies lie. The second interment on the register is that of Edward S. Fisher, a sergeant of Company "D," 40th New York infantry regiment.

Thus the wearers of blue and gray dissolved all differences in death and lay down to their long sleep indifferent to the success alike of North or South.

These first graves were not allowed to remain unmolested, for after the Secretary of War had approved the action of the Quartermaster-General, and ordered that the grounds should be used thenceforth for cemeterial purposes, these first buried bodies were reinterred in the lower cemetery marked section "A" on the map of Arlington, and the bodies of commissioned officers were buried along the terrace.

The cemetery being now regularly established, a reliable and intelligent sexton was placed in charge; neat, if not substantial, headboards were placed at every grave containing all obtainable information concerning the occupant, and everything possible done to dispel the feeling, still existent, that the soldiers dying at Washington were irreverently and negligently treated. From the 13th of May, 1864, the burials at Arlington were constant and many. Every day the gloomy black ambulances, laden with corpses enclosed in common pine coffins, made their way along the dusty highway from the Aqueduct to the gates of Arlington. In the two months and a half from May 13 to June 30, 1864, the interments at Arlington numbered 2,619; 231 of those buried being colored soldiers. From this time on the work of burying the bodies of those who died in the hospitals at Washington was carried steadily on at Arlington until the close of the war, in April, 1865. The interments to June 30, 1865, numbered 5,291. Before the war had been concluded, however, the idea of establishing national cemeteries at convenient points had been developed until there were a large number located about Washington. In consequence the interments at Arlington for this year do not represent all the deaths in Washington hospitals, for the terrible record of mortality shows that 15,708 heroes yielded up their lives during the year ending June 30, 1865, in the hospital wards of the National Capital; a number whose appalling magnitude does not force itself upon the imagination until it is remembered that this great total of male adults represents the population of a large city.

In this year the work of establishing new national cemeteries and improving those already established went forward with great strides. A grateful country now had full leisure to appreciate the great debt it owed to the men who had laid down their lives in their country's defence, and took such steps as would best demonstrate the desire felt to express a nation's gratitude and remembrance. At Arlington everything possible was done to restore to the place its natural beauty and former grandeur of forested hills and sloping lawns. The splendid oak groves immediately surrounding the mansion had not fallen before the devastating scythe of war, and thus the great element of the natural and familiar aspect of the place had been preserved. As far as possible the estate was restored to its pristine condition, and the old mansion, dismantled of its priceless treasures but still preserving its classical and dignified architectural beauty, was given over to the superintendent of the cemetery as his quarters. Terraces battered down by the constant trampling of man and horse and utterly denuded of turf were built up and resodded, and the long sloping hill, stretching away to the south, scarred by drain pits and camp-fire sites, was leveled and planted with groves of ornamental trees. Drives were restored, and emerald lawns again stretched away in velvety beauty from the portico of the mansion. As far as possible the scars of war were obliterated, and in a few short months the place again resumed the quiet beauty it had known as the homestead of Custis. The sturdy forests by the river side, however, could not be restored, and the beautiful surroundings of the far-famed Custis Spring became but a memory. In the immediate vicinity of the house, however, a perfect restoration was possible, so that in the latter part of 1865 those who had known the place before the internecine strife would not have noted any great changes save for the long lines of white headboards that gleamed through the vistas of forest aisles on every hand.

Near the battle-fields of Spottsylvania and the Wilderness the national cemeteries were established during this year in which were interred the remains of those who fell in these battles and were not accorded proper burial at the time. Capt. Moore, with a detail of men, was sent into this region on the 12th of June, 1865, and was engaged during the rest of the month in collecting the remains of Union soldiers and reinterring them in the newly-established cemeteries. A careful and thorough search was made and all bodies found were buried under the direction of Capt.

Moore, and headboards bearing the name, rank, and regiment of those reinterred were placed at each grave.

At the Wilderness two national cemeteries were established, cemetery No. 1 being on the Orange Court-House turnpike, about two miles from the Wilderness tavern; cemetery No. 2 being located on the Orange Court-House plank road, about 2½ miles from its junction with the turnpike.

At Spottsylvania few bodies were found uninterred, the dead of both armies having been buried by a Mr. Sanford, having a farm in that region. These, however, were disinterred and buried in the new national cemetery established there.

The work of repair on the old Soldiers' Home cemetery was completed in this year. This practically comprised the cemeterial work done in the early part of 1865.

During the year ending June 30, 1866, the Quartermaster-General's office continued to carry on the work of collecting into national cemeteries the remains of those who fell in battle or died in the cause of the Union. At the end of the fiscal year, forty-one of these cemeteries had been established, and ten more had been decided upon. Ground was purchased, wherever practicable, on or at least near the great battle-fields, and dedicated as national cemeteries. Some of these cemeteries, as shown in the case of Arlington, were created during the war; Gettysburg, for instance, at whose dedication, November 19, 1863, Lincoln delivered his memorable address, having been commenced comparatively early in the war. The majority came into existence in the years immediately subsequent, being filled in many cases with the bodies of those who were removed from the hastily excavated graves on the battle-fields. This work of collecting the bodies from the battle-fields was continued in this year under the direction of Brevet Brigadier-General J. J. Dana.

At this time there were 412 cemeteries, not the property of the nation, in which loyal soldiers were buried to the number of 237,142. The national cemeteries contained at this time 104,528 bodies, aggregating, with those buried in other cemeteries, 341,670. Of these, it was possible to identify only 202,761, it being utterly impossible to identify 138,901 bodies. There were besides in the national cemeteries the remains of 13,657 rebel prisoners. The total expenses incurred by the Government in procuring proper burial for these remains amounted to $1,144,791, while it was estimated that $1,609,294 would be required to complete the work.

As stated before, the work of collecting the dead from the battle-fields was carried forward in this year. The actual operations in the department of Washington were under the superintendence of Col. M. G. Ludington, chief quartermaster, assisted by Capt. John R. Hynes and Brevet Major James Gleason, assistant quartermaster. These officers, besides having the care of the cemeteries at Annapolis and Point Lookout, Maryland, containing 2,675 and 3,523 graves respectively, were entrusted with the disinterment of all bodies buried on the battle-fields of Maryland and Virginia within a circuit of thirty-five miles from Washington. All these bodies were reinterred at Arlington. To Col. Ludington was also assigned the work of reinterring the bodies from the line of the Orange and Alexandria railroad as far south as Orange Court-House, and from the district tributary to that road on each side, extending half-way to the line of the Richmond and Fredericksburg railroad on the east and to the Blue Ridge on the west. The bodies north of the Rappahannock river were removed to Arlington Cemetery, those south of the Rappahannock being interred in the cemetery established at Culpeper Court-House.

A vault in this same year was constructed at Arlington under the superintendence of Col. Ludington, to which were removed such scattered and disorganized remains from the battle-fields of Bull Run and Manassas as could not be identified for separate burial.

Perhaps no work ever before attempted by an army officer presented such gruesome and uncanny features as this labor of collecting from the fields of strife and carnage these poor dismembered fragments of human skeletons that were once swadded, perhaps, in the huge muscle and sinew of some titanic hero who dashed forward into the very heart of death's kingdom with bayonet fixed and the warrior's cry of battle ringing from his lips. Some fierce, wild struggle, worthy the tribute of a laureate's pen, would be but vaguely imagined in a group of bleached skeletons hidden in some fence corner, with bare desiccated bones fractured by splintering shell or pierced by stinging bullet. In sequestered nooks in the pine and cedar growth of the forests of this region a few grim relics of man's mortality would tell a story of heroic deeds more glorious than the achievements of mailed knights; the sortie by night and the ambushed surprise, with the hopeless battling against invincible odds; the gallant company encompassed by battalions and brigades and fighting till the last cartridge exploded and then waiting death and oblivion with fast-gripped bayoneted rifles and the courage that made of our country a land of god-like heroes. These were the stories the mute witnesses told; not in the well-rounded sentences of the historian or the spirited verse of the poet, but in a language as easy to understand. Throughout all this region the fighting had been of the severest kind; roaring parks of artillery had flung the death-dealing shell with frightful accuracy, and at every point the hand-to-hand conflict had left the story of its terrible intensity in the massed bodies of the mangled dead.

At times a tale both pitiful and tragic would be told by the solitary skeleton of some lone picket who had fallen at his post without having been able to fire a shot in his own defence.

In all these cases identification was impossible. When in the sharp conflict of armies one gave way and retreated the other followed fast without much heed for the brave fellows who had dropped from the company's rolls. In such cases, unless buried by some unselfish Samaritan, the bodies lay in the bleaching sun and rain, the flesh torn away by the carrion fowls, until only the fiercely grinning skull and brightly-polished frame of bone remained. In many cases, to the glory of the Union army be it said, skeletons with U. S. accoutrements were found in the abatis of rebel earthworks, where they had been carried by the impetus of some wild charge and left by their comrades when they fell death-stricken by the fierce fire from above.

The collection of these scattered remains was certainly not a pleasant duty. Day after day the party, in charge of Col. Ludington, went carefully over the ground that had been occupied by the contending armies, finding at times clustered groups of complete skeletons, and again searching closely through wide fields only to find a pierced skull, or a few mere fragments. Some crimson-flowered vine clambering in rank luxuriance along the zig-zag fence-lines into some wild, lonely nook in the gloomy pineries would, if followed back to earth, be found rioting in the rich mold whose fertility was derived from near-lying, unburied bodies of the country's loyal dead.

As far as possible, the bones belonging to one individual were collected and shipped to Arlington in small wooden cases about two feet long by a foot square. Often a body would be represented by a skull or thigh-bone; again by nearly a full complement.

When the work was finished, 2,111 oblong wooden cases, representing this number of human beings, had been placed in the vault at Arlington. Afterwards a granite sarcophagus of simple but impressive beauty was placed over this vault, and is to-day one of the most interesting objects at Arlington. It bears the simple inscription :-

Here lie the bones of 2,111 unknown soldiers. Their remains could not be identified, but their names and deaths are recorded in the archives of their country, and its grateful citizens honor them as of their noble army of martyrs. May they rest in peace.

Besides this work Col. Ludington and Capt. John R. Hynes also were assigned, as stated before, the task of removing to Arlington the dead bodies disinterred in Maryland within a circuit of thirty-five miles from Washington. A numbered list of these exhumations was prepared by Capt. Hynes, who also made a great number of sketches of the various localities whence the bodies were taken. Figures were marked on the sketches to correspond with those on the lists, the latter giving in each case the location of the body as reinterred at Arlington. The lists and sketch-books were placed on file in Washington on the completion of the work and led to the identification of many of these bodies, particularly in the case of those marked "unknown." In all cases, whether the bodies were known or unknown, the locality from which they were removed, together with the date of removal, was placed upon the headboards.

The total number of bodies of United States soldiers buried in the department of Washington under the charge of Col. Ludington in this year was 5,287, of which number 4,180 were finally identified. The total number of interments in the department of Washington at this time was as follows :

1. United States Military Asylum, 5,717 graves.
2. Harmony National Cemetery, 3,251 graves.

3. Battle Cemetery, 40 graves.
4. Union Cemetery, 1,012 graves.
5. Arlington, 9,795 graves.
6. Alexandria Cemetery, 3,601 graves.
Total number of graves 23,416.

During the years 1866, '67, '68, '69, and '70 the work of the cemeterial branch of the Quartermaster-General's office was carried steadily forward, and the report for the latter year shows that but little remained to be accomplished. The labors of this division were virtually completed. Occasionally bodies were found after this lapse of years, but they were few in number and were removed as soon as discovered to the nearest national cemetery.

Plans for beautifying the cemeteries by planting shrubs and ornamental trees were carried into effect during this year. At Arlington and four other cemeteries handsome arched gateways were erected, and the Arlington cemetery was also improved by the construction of a stone wall entirely enclosing the portion set aside for burial purposes at that time.

During the year the interments of Union dead throughout the country numbered 315,555; of this number, 143,446 being unidentified.

Prior to 1869 twenty-one volumes of the Roll of Honor, containing the record of 255,655 of deceased Union soldiers, were published, and in this year four volumes were added containing the record of 77,300 graves.

During the year 1870 the work of improving Arlington was continued, many interments being made. At the close of the fiscal year 15,932 graves were located within the enclosed grounds.

During the year 1871 many improvements in the grounds at Arlington were mapped out and carried into effect. A large and imposing entrance gate of Seneca stone was erected. A "sylvan grove" of maples was planted in the southwest portion of the grounds, on the plan of a Gothic cathedral, with arched avenues leading away in all directions.

In the year 1872 the Quartermaster-General decided upon the form of headstone now in use, and for the first time the plain plank headboards were removed and the substantial slabs of granite and marble that now mark each soldier's grave were placed in all the cemeteries.

From this time on until the year 1892 the history of Arlington is too uneventful, aside from the legal battle for its possession, to deserve a detailed chronicle. As the years passed, the white headstones increased in number and the city of the dead grew in population. No great changes came, however. A wide section was set aside for the burial of the officers of the army and navy, to the west of the mansion, and only lately two interments have been made on the sloping lawn in front of the house. These graves contain the bodies of Gen. Sheridan and Admiral Porter, and it has always been the hope of the American people that the body of Grant would rest with these at Arlington. Within a year the stone wall enclosing that portion of Arlington set aside for burial purposes has been moved and run further to the south so as to enclose the old earthworks known as Fort McPherson.

This addition will give nearly 100 acres more for burials. The land is entirely clear, the great forest belt that extended along the plateau having been cut away, both to the west and south, when Forts Whipple and McPherson were established.

During the past summer the laboring force at Arlington, under the superintendence of landscape gardener Rhodes, has transformed the old dismantled earthwork south of the cemetery proper into a fair semblance of the sturdy structure that stood there during the war. Moat, bastions, and parapet cleanly clad in velvety turf, with sharp angles and smooth flat surfaces rising from the surrounding sward, will bring back to every soldier and veteran of the late war long dead memories of the days when behind every such embankment lay massed troops and heavy pieces of ordnance ready for the terrible earnest work before them.

Fort McPherson *redivivus* is far handsomer than the old Fort McPherson, designed for purely utilitarian purposes. The lines of the latter in their mathematical accuracy have not been disturbed, but sodded slopes now face the invader where in time of war there was only the bare yellow clay, revetted in places by planking and timbers. The sharp edges of the bastions, too, are outlined with a care and delicacy that, while adding to the beauty of the place, detracts in some sense from the feeling of realism induced by a sight of this restored relic of the time of Washington's greatest danger. The fort, however, will be an object-lesson to the thousands who visit it and will in all probability form one of the objects of greatest interest to the average visitor.

Superintendent J. A. Commerford has entire charge of the national cemetery at Arlington, having been appointed to his present position about six years ago by the War Department. Superintendent Commerford has a force of fourteen laborers constantly employed on the grounds, and has, besides, the direction of the operations of the special force that for some time past has been at work on the restoration of Fort McPherson. Landscape gardener D. H. Rhodes has charge of the floral display, and under the direction of the superintendent supervises all work connected with improvements on or about the grounds. Nearly all the workmen employed are ex-Union soldiers. One of them, however, is an old negro, Wesley Norris, one of the slaves of Mr. Custis, who was born on the estate and often accompanied his master on his long hunting expeditions. He was one of the squad of slaves that bore the body of the first master of Arlington House to his lonely grave in the deep grove west of the mansion, now marked by a crumbling stone shaft.

CHAPTER VII.

THE GOVERNMENT'S TITLE TO ARLINGTON AND HOW OBTAINED—INTERESTING LEGAL DOCUMENTS.

The story of the passage of the Arlington estate from the possession of the Lees to that of the United States Government is not the least interesting portion of the story of this historic old place. In the very first days of the war, as already shown, it was occupied by the Union forces and never after ceased to be occupied and used by the United States. In January, 1864, the Government secured what was deemed a good title to the estate by purchase at a sale in accordance with the provisions of the direct tax-act. August 5, 1861, the Government, in order to raise sufficient funds to carry on the war, passed "An act to provide increased revenues from imports to pay interest on the public debt, and for other purposes." Section 8 of this act provided for the levying of a direct tax upon the United States annually of $20,000,000, apportioned among the several States. Virginia's share of the direct tax amounted to $937,550.66$\frac{2}{3}$.

On June 7, 1862, an act was passed providing for the collection of the direct taxes in the insurrectionary districts within the United States. It had been ascertained long before this that it was impossible to collect the taxes, levied by the direct tax act, in the States at this time in open rebellion. This act provided that when, by reason of insurrection in any State, the civil authority became obstructed and the act providing for the collection of the direct tax could not be peacefully executed, the tax apportionment should be charged or apportioned in each insurrectionary district upon all lands and lots of ground according to the enumeration and valuation of the last assessment preceding the breaking out of the war. The act provided further for the sale of all such tracts or parcels of land in order to secure the payment of this tax, and set forth at great length the manner in which such sale should be conducted. Commissioners were appointed whose duty it should be to apportion the assessments and conduct the sales according to the provisions of the act. A final section of the bill read as follows:

And provided further, That at such sale any tracts, parcels, or lots of land which may be selected under the direction of the President for Government use for war, military, naval, revenue, charitable, educational, or police purposes, may at said sale be bid in by said commissioners, under the direction of the President, for and struck off to the United States.

On the 6th of February an act was passed to amend "An act for the collection of direct taxes in the insurrectionary districts." This act, based upon the failures and mistakes of the former act, contained detailed and specific instructions as to the manner in which such sales should be conducted.

Under the provisions of these acts and the amendments thereto the sale of the Arlington estate on the 11th of January, 1864, was advertised in the *Virginia State Journal* from the 21st of November, 1863, the date of the first insertion, until the day preceding the sale. In January, 1864, Arlington was occupied by two forts, with full garrisons and thousands of tents. In consequence, the Secretary of War recommended to the President that the estate be purchased by the U. S. Government for military purposes. President Lincoln acted on this recommendation, and on the 11th of January, 1864, the estate of 1,100 acres was put up at public sale, and after but little competition was bid in and struck off to the United States by the order of the President, acting in accordance with the provisions of the act cited above. The amount of the Government's purchasing bid was $26,100. The estate had been assessed the year previous to the breaking out of the war at $34,100.

The three commissioners for Virginia who had charge of the sale of the Arlington estate were John Hawxhurst, Gilbert F. Watson, and A. Lawrence Foster. By reason of some remissness the certificate of this tax sale was not made out until September 26, 1866, the year after the war closed.

From this time on the Government held possession under the tax-sale title. In May, 1864, burials of Union soldiers were made on the place and shortly after it was established as a national cemetery.

Neither Gen. Lee nor his wife, Mary Custis Lee, made any attempt to regain possession of the Arlington property. They were but life tenants and had no title to the property, which had been devised by George Washington Parke Custis to his grandson,

George Washington Custis Lee, by the terms of his will, which read as follows:

WILL OF G. W. P. CUSTIS.

In the name of God, amen. I, George Washington Parke Custis, of Arlington House, in the county of Alexandria and State of Virginia, being sound in body and mind, do make and ordain this instrument of writing as my last will and testament, revoking all other wills and testaments whatever. I give and bequeath to my dearly beloved daughter and only child, Mary Ann Randolph Lee, my Arlington House estate, in the county of Alexandria and State of Virginia, containing eleven hundred acres, more or less, and my mill on Four-Mile Run, in the county of Alexandria, and the lands of mine adjacent to said mill, in the counties of Alexandria and Fairfax, in the State of Virginia, the use and benefit of all just mentioned during the term of her natural life, together with my horses and carriages, furniture, pictures, and plate, during the term of her natural life.

On the death of my daughter, Mary Ann Randolph Lee, all the property left to her during the term of her natural life I give and bequeath to my eldest grandson, George Washington Custis Lee, to him and his heirs forever, he, my said eldest grandson, taking my name and arms.

I leave and bequeath to my four granddaughters, Mary, Ann, Agnes, and Mildred Lee, to each ten thousand dollars. I give and bequeath to my second grandson, William Henry Fitzhugh Lee, when he shall be of age, my estate called the White House, in the county of New Kent and State of Virginia, containing four thousand acres, more or less, to him and his heirs forever.

I give and bequeath to my third and youngest grandson, Robert Edward Lee, when he is of age, my estate in the county of King William and State of Virginia, called Romancock, containing four thousand acres, more or less, to him and his heirs forever.

My estate of Smith's Island, at the capes of Virginia, and in the county of Northampton, I leave to be sold to assist in paying my granddaughters' legacies, to be sold in such manner as may be deemed by my executors most expedient.

Any and all lands that I may possess in the counties of Stafford, Richmond, and Westmoreland, I leave to be sold to aid in paying my granddaughters' legacies.

I give and bequeath my lot in square No. 21, Washington city, to my son-in-law, Lieut. Col. Robert E. Lee, to him and his heirs forever. My daughter, Mary A. R. Lee, has the privilege, by this will, of dividing my family plate among my grandchildren, but the Mt. Vernon altogether, and every article I possess relating to Washington and that came from Mt. Vernon is to remain with my daughter at Arlington House during said daughter's life, and at her death to go to my eldest grandson, George Washington Custis Lee, and to descend from him entire and unchanged to my latest posterity.

My estates of the White House, in the county of New Kent, and Romancock, in the county of King William, both being in the State of Virginia, together with Smith's Island, and the lands I may possess in the counties of Stafford, Richmond, and Westmoreland counties are charged with the payment of the legacies of my granddaughters.

Smith's Island and the aforesaid lands in Stafford, Richmond, and Westmoreland only are to be sold, the lands of the White House and Romancock to be worked to raise the aforesaid legacies to my four granddaughters.

And upon the legacies to my four granddaughters being paid, and my estates that are required to pay the said legacies being clear of debt, then I give freedom to my slaves, the said slaves to be emancipated by my executors in such manner as to my executors may seem most expedient and proper, the said emancipation to be accomplished in not exceeding five years from the time of my decease.

And I do constitute and appoint as my executors Lieut. Col. Robert Edward Lee, Robert Lee Randolph, of Eastern View, Rt. Rev. Bishop Meade, and George Washington Peter.

This will, written by my hand, is signed, sealed, and executed the twenty-sixth day of March, eighteen hundred and fifty-five.

GEORGE WASHINGTON PARKE CUSTIS. [SEAL.]

26th March, 1855.
Witness:
   MARTHA CUSTIS WILLIAMS.
   M. EUGENE WEBSTER.

George Washington Custis Lee did not take the name and arms of Custis as required, so in order to quiet the claims of the other heirs and to secure to G. W. C. Lee the property devised to him by his grandfather Mrs. Lee left at her death the following will:

WILL OF MARY C. LEE.

In the name of God, amen. I, Mary Custis Lee, widow of General Robert E. Lee, do make, publish, and declare this as my last will and testament.

In compliance with the wishes expressed in the last will and testament of my deceased husband, Robert E. Lee, and by virtue of the power and authority therein conferred upon me, I appoint and direct as follows:

First. That owing to an arrangement between my children satisfactory to them, and my sons W. H. F. Lee and Robert E. Lee having in writing relinquished all benefit, present or prospective, in the estate of their father, Robert E. Lee, deceased, it is my will and desire, in view of said agreement and relinquishment, that the said W. H. F. Lee and Robert E. Lee be excluded from any participation in the estate of said Robert E. Lee, deceased.

Second. It is my will and desire, and I do so appoint and direct, that all of the estate of the said Robert E. Lee shall, upon my decease, be equally divided between my son G. W. Custis Lee and my three daughters, Mary, Mildred, and Agnes, share and share alike, each taking one equal fourth part.

Third. Should my son, G. W. Custis Lee, recover the estate called Arlington situate in the county of Alexandria, Va., or be paid therefor by the Government of the United States, then, and in that event, it is my will and desire, and I so appoint and direct, that the one-fourth part of his father's estate given to him, the said G. Custis Lee, in the foregoing clause of my will, shall pass and belong to my three daughters above named, in equal portions.

I appoint my sons G. W. Custis Lee and W. H. F. Lee executors of this my last will and testament without security.

Given under my hand and seal this 9th day of June, A. D. 1873.

MARY CUSTIS LEE.

Witnesses:
   A. M. LEE.
   FRANCIS G. SMITH.

By the provisions of these wills Mr. George Washington Custis Lee became the sole claimant to the Arlington estate, and took the first steps to secure possession, or at least a fair compensation for the loss of the estate, by filing in the circuit court of Alexandria a suit in ejectment against Frederick Kauffman and R. P. Strong, parties occupying the ground as representatives of the Government. Mr. Kauffman was at that time superintendent of the national cemetery at Arlington, which contained not more than 200 acres. R. P. Strong was the commanding officer at Fort Whipple, now Fort Myer, then the home of the Signal Corps of the Army. These proceedings in ejectment also included about 200 negroes, residents of Freedman's village, who were permitted to hold small tracts of land on the Arlington estate in return for which privilege they were expected to work a certain number of hours each day at the fort. Early in the proceedings, however, an order was issued dismissing the suit against these negroes, as it was clearly shown that they were simply tenants of Commandant Strong.

Action was commenced in the circuit court of Alexandria on the first Monday in May, 1877, but was, as soon as the declaration was filed, removed by writ of certiorari to the circuit court of the United States for the eastern district of Virginia, where all the subsequent proceedings took place.

After a long though interesting hearing a verdict in favor of the plaintiff was rendered.

Although the United States had not appeared as a party to the suit in the court below, the case was carried to the Supreme Court on a writ of error, based on the rejection of a suggestion submitted during the hearing in the inferior court by the Attorney-General moving the withdrawal of the action, inasmuch as the United States had established its claim to the land involved by a ten-years holding and a valid title conferred by the tax sale.

The appeal was heard during the October term of the Supreme Court, 1882, and was argued by Wm. D. Shipman, A. Ferguson Beach, and Wm. J. Roberts for the defendant, and Solicitor Westell Willoughby for the Government. The decision, which was rendered by Justice Miller, held briefly that the court below had no jurisdiction in the case, and the verdict, therefore, could not hold. The suit in ejectment against Strong and Kauffman, it was shown, was really a suit against the United States, and as a sovereign cannot be sued without his consent, the Supreme Court held that the lower court had acted without authority, inasmuch as it had no power to render judgment where it could not enforce execution.

This decision, however, granted the validity of the title of Mr. Lee to the estate and left the National Government in the position of holding possession of the estate involved by barring the claimant from further action in the courts. It was fully understood, however, that the Government could have no just t'le to the estate and the Secretary of War was in consequence directed by a resolution of Congress to ascertain upon what terms a valid title to the property could be secured. He accordingly confer. with Mr. Lee, who expressed his willingness to yield all claims to the Arlington estate and deed the same to the United States for the sum of $150,000.

On transmitting this information to Congress a clause was embodied in the general deficiency bill, passed March 3, 1883, appropriating the sum named. The clause carrying the appropriation reads as follows :

To enable the Secretary of War to remove all claims and pretensions in respect of the property in the State of Virginia known as Arlington, on which a cemetery for the burial of deceased soldiers of the United States has been established, and which property was taken by the United States for public use in the year anno Domini eighteen hundred and sixty-four, one hundred and fifty thousand dollars ; but this appropriation shall not be paid out of the Treasury until the Attorney-General shall be satisfied, and so certify to the Secretary of War, that the deed or deeds to be given to the United States to the end aforesaid will convey a complete title and contain covenants of general warranty and covenants against every manner of claim against or in respect of said property, whether in rem or in personam, and also against all and every claim for damages in respect of, or the use and occupation of, said property, and also a release by every person entitled of all claim for and to the amount bid, or any part thereof, in behalf of the United States, on the tax sale of said property.

A deed to the property in question was promptly executed by Mr. Lee and presented to the Attorney-General for his approval. The latter, acting in accordance with the provisions of the act making the appropriation, examined closely into Mr. Lee's title to the Arlington property, and after assuring himself that the deed conveyed a complete warranty against every manner of claim against the property forwarded to the Secretary of War a lengthy opinion in which he reviewed the legal history of the suits for recovery and the title of the claimant to the property. This title of Mr. Lee was found to be without flaw, and the deed submitted by him fulfilled all the requirements of the provisions of the act of March 3d. Accordingly the opinion of the Attorney-General concludes with the statement: "Therefore I am of the opinion that the deed of Mr. Lee may properly be accepted upon the terms proposed." Upon the receipt of the opinion of Attorney-General Brewster Secretary Lincoln ordered the Secretary of the Treasury to make the payment provided for in the appropriation. Shortly after, Mr. Lee received the sum of $150,000 from the Treasury Department and the United States came into possession of a perfect and flawless title to the Arlington House estate.

The authors of this work, at great labor and expense, have obtained the following document showing the manner in which the lands under discussion have changed owners from the days of Gov. Berkeley in 1669 to the present time:

"An abstract of title to the Arlington House estate, a tract of land containing about 1,100 acres, situate in Alexandria county, formerly Fairfax county, State of Virginia. The land was a part of the grant or patent from Sir William Berkeley, Governor of Virginia, to Robert Howser, dated October 21, 1669, under which John and Gerard Alexander asserted title as late as 1735. In the case of Birch v. Alexander, 1. Wash. (Va.) R. 34, this grant was maintained by the court of appeals.

Gerard Alexander, by his will, dated August 9, 1760, devised the same to his son Gerard. Vide Will Book B, p. 327, Fairfax county records. Gerard Alexander and Jane, his wife, conveyed the same to John Parke Custis by deed, dated December 25, A. D. 1778. The general index shows that such a deed was recorded Liber N, Fairfax county records, but, with other records of that county, was lost or destroyed during the late war. A certified copy of the original deed has been preserved and is submitted with this abstract for delivery to the United States as a muniment of title. Pursuant to a decree of Fairfax county court dated June 21, 1796, in a suit wherein the representatives of John Parke Custis were complainants and the heirs of Gerard Alexander were defendants, the portion of Gerard Alexander, Jr., in the lands of his father were allotted to the legal representati of the said John Parke Custis. The record of this suit was, however, lost or destroyed in the late war.

John Parke Custis died, intestate, on the 5th of November, A. D. 1781, ætat 28. The law of primogeniture was then in force, and this estate descended to his only son, George W. P. Custis. As to the time of his death, Irving's 'Life of Washington,' vol. 4, p. 358, and a certificate of the clerk of Fairfax county show that administration of his estate had been granted by that court prior to February 20, 1782.

Primogeniture in Virginia was abolished by an act passed October, 1785, to take effect January 1, 1787. (Hening's Statutes, vol. 12, p. 138.) George Washington Parke Custis died seized and possessed of this estate in 1857. By his will, dated March 26, 1855, it was devised to his only child, Mary Ann Randolph Lee, for life, remainder in fee to his 'eldest grandson, George W. C. Lee, to him and his heirs forever, he, my said eldest grandson, taking my name and arms' (Will Book No. 7, p. 267, Alexandria county court), and for copy of said will and decree admitting same to probate vide record of the case, The United States v. G. W. C. Lee, pp. 74-75.

In that suit it was proved that Geo. Wash. Parke Custis had possessed and lived upon the estate for more than 35 years, prior to its institution, and by the land books of the county that the estate had been listed and assessed for taxation as the property of Geo. W. P. Custis during his lifetime, and he was born prior to 1780.

Mrs. M. A. R. Lee, the tenant for life, died in 1873, and as G. W. C. Lee did not take the name and arms of his grandfather, to avoid any question of his title, his heirs, who were the children of Mrs. Lee, waived in a release any claim they might have to the whole. (Vide Liber B, No. 4, folio 114, Alexandria County Court; also record of above-mentioned suit, pp. 78 and 79.)

The estate was held and possessed by Mrs. Lee until 1861, since which period the United States has held it in possession, and since 1864, when it was held for direct taxes, has claimed it as absolute owner."

CHAPTER VIII.

THE NATIONAL CEMETERY—A GENERAL DESCRIPTION OF ARLINGTON, WITH AN ACCOUNT OF SOME OF THE DISTINGUISHED SOLDIERS BURIED THERE.

The cemetery as it appears to the visitor now presents, seemingly, endless vistas of marble headstones, stretching out in unbroken lines like the silent army of the dead standing in review before the succeeding generation of the living. Notwithstanding this, however, only a small portion of the ground enclosed within the walls of Arlington is occupied by graves. The rest is still taken up with the sloping lawns and groves of magnificent oaks, with here and there bits of wild wood, as yet unadorned by the art of the landscape gardener.

The main entrances to the grounds are along the Georgetown and Alexandria road, which skirts the hills of the cemetery and winds its way along the level ground below. Here there are three gates, flanked by columns and ornamented by arches, and a fourth, known as the new gate, which swings between massive piles of masonry that once formed a portion of the old War Department building. The first of these gates is the Ord and Weitzel gate. On either side is a tall column surmounted by a funeral urn, and on the columns are inscribed the names of Gens. Ord and Weitzel. Lower down the road is a larger and more imposing entrance, known as the Sheridan gate. Here there are four columns supporting a moulded cross-piece of stone. The name Sheridan stands out in bold relief from the masonry, and on each of the four columns is a distinguished name. The names are Scott, Lincoln, Stanton, and Grant. The third gate is the McClellan gate. At this the entrance to the grounds is marked by a massive structure of red sandstone, artistic in its design and imposing in its strength and beauty. Over the gateway is the name of the conqueror at the battle of Antietam, and beneath it an appropriate inscription. The fourth gate is a new gate, very simple in its design and as yet but little used.

From each of these gates roadways winding through beautiful

groves of trees lead to the mansion. From the Ord and Weitzel gate the road takes the visitor through a narrow strip of ground in which the first burials during the war were made. The strip contains not more than an acre or two, but in it are about 5,000 graves. It terminates in a narrow point formed by the road and the stone wall of the cemetery, and above this point is a large circular bed of flowers Passing the flowers, the road plunges suddenly into a wood so dense and wild that one wonders if the peaceful little burying-ground through which he has passed can have any connection with the great national cemetery. Proceeding, this feeling of wonder increases as along hillsides and through deep ravines the road winds its way, flanked all the time by sturdy oaks and a dense undergrowth of saplings, till suddenly, after a steep climb, it emerges from the natural forest into the area of well-cared-for grounds about the stately old mansion.

The roads that lead up from the other gates have about them none of the wild beauty that marks the thoroughfare just described, but they are none the less beautiful. They pass beneath the spreading branches of gigantic oaks, and wind about on terraces, flanked by smooth rolling lawns. The grounds through which they pass formed originally the park of the Custis estate, and few changes have been made in them since the good-natured founder of the place put them in shape. The Government has improved the roads and smoothed down the rough places, but the natural beauty of the place remains as it was when Custis, as a young man, first erected Arlington House. At intervals along both roads huge blocks of hewn stone are found which were placed in their present positions years ago and used as seats by Custis and his friends.

All the roads, no matter at what place the entrance to the grounds is made, lead to but one central point, the picturesque old house. It stands embowered in virgin trees, the most interesting feature still of the vast resting-place of the dead, while ranged about it, in shady wood or sunny dell, the myriads of graves seem fittingly to harmonize with thoughts of its departed greatness. Some description of the old mansion has heretofore been given, and as it stands to-day exactly as it did in the time of Parke Custis there seems little need to repeat it.

The change from the past to the present is shown in the interior of the house. Blank, cheerless walls greet one where, in years gone by, hung objects of artistic value, while the bare rooms can now give but little idea of the life and cheerfulness that once reigned there.

Over the main entrance to the building hangs a sign, "Superintendent's Office," and the door on the right that opens from the hallway leads to the apartments occupied by that official. The upper floor of the building and the entire right wing are taken up by the superintendent's apartments, and are not open to the public. The rooms on the left are always open, but they possess very little of interest.

A few shields, bearing appropriate inscriptions; pictures of two or three different sections of the grounds; the great Decoration Day orations of President Lincoln and Robert G. Ingersoll set in frames, and a desk, at which visitors are requested to register their names in a large book that lies upon it, are all that they contain.

Directly in front of the main entrance stands the flag-pole, and on the hill beside it are the graves of the two illustrious commanders, Gen. P. H. Sheridan and Admiral Porter. The Admiral's grave is to the left and is still unmarked by stone of any kind. A fence of chains surrounds it and indicates the space where, in the near future, a monument worthy of the dead man's fame will be erected.

Over the grave of Gen. Sheridan stands the most beautiful monument at Arlington. It is a block of highly polished granite. Upon its face is a bronze flag and medallion, the latter containing a head of the dead general in high relief. The bronze cast is the work of Samuel Kitson, of Boston, and has been greatly admired as a likeness of Gen. Sheridan. The grave itself is overgrown with ivy, and is enclosed by a chain suspended from pillars of stone.

On the same slope and but a few yards distant from the grave of Sheridan is the grave of Surg.-Gen. Jedediah Hyde Baxter, whose death occurred in December, 1890. This grave is also surmounted by a handsome monument. Other graves on this hillside are those of Bvt. Maj.-Gen. J. H. Mower and Gen. Samuel David Sturgis.

It is the intention of the War Department to reserve the slope on which these graves are located as the burial-place of highly-distinguished officers of either the Army or Navy. As yet the graves mentioned are the only ones it contains, but the remains of Gen. Crook will before long be included in the number. At present Gen. Crook is buried in what is known as the officers' section. The section set apart for the burial of officers lies along the level ridge that extends back from the mansion, in the direction of Fort Myer. It is divided by a roadway into two portions, and is separated from the general burying-ground by the road that leads from the Fort Myer gate, past the rostrum and amphitheatre, to the Arlington house. Here lie many distinguished officers who served their country bravely, and over their remains stand handsome monuments of sombre granite and glistening marble. It is the one spot in the cemetery where any departure from the simple style of gravestone provided by the Government has been permitted, and as a result the spot is rapidly becoming one of the most beautiful to be found there. No attempt at uniformity in the style of these monuments has been attempted, but loving friends and admiring comrades have been allowed to exercise their fancy in the erection of these testimonials of regard.

The most ornate marble shafts are to be found here bearing inscriptions that show the services rendered by the dead heroes and the esteem of those who served with them, while equally conspicuous by their simplicity are the rough-hewn blocks of granite that mark many of the graves. The latter, indeed, predominate, and a striking feature of this part of the cemetery is the absence of all ostentatious display about the memorials reared to perpetuate the fame of those who rest beneath them. The rough-hewn granite blocks, the undressed shafts bearing upon their faces but the name and rank of the dead soldier, are suggestive in their simplicity of the rugged, forceful character of the men who planned campaigns and led their troops to battle. They are as if death had stripped commanders of all the gaudy trappings of war and now hold up, for veneration and respect, the simple man beneath. Here lie the venerable Harney, the courageous Paul, the dashing Ricketts, the indefatigable Crook, the resourceful Meigs, the gallant Belknap, and many others, whose records both in peace and war entitle them to the grateful remembrance of their countrymen.

An object of general interest to visitors is the sarcophagus of dressed marble which contains the bodies of Gen. M. C. Meigs,

Quartermaster-General of the army during the entire civil war, and of his wife, Louisa Rogers Meigs. About this are the graves of other members of the Meigs family. At one side of the sarcophagus is the grave of Lieut. John Rogers Meigs, the eldest son of Gen. Meigs, who was killed in battle in 1864. The young man was chief of engineers in the Army of the Shenandoah. A rectangular block of black marble, on which rests a bronze figure of the young soldier as he was found on the battle-field, marks the grave. On the other side of the sarcophagus, marked by a simple shaft of stone, is the grave of Gen. Meigs' father, Josiah Meigs, who was Commissioner of the General Land Office in the early years of the century. Two children of Gen. Meigs, Charles D. and Vincent Trowbridge Meigs, are also buried near. Not far from this group of graves is a marble slab over the last resting-place of Col. John McComb, an able officer, and for years before the war one of that distinguished group of friends that included Lee, Johnston, Meigs, and others.

An undressed granite shaft half enveloped in clinging ivy rears its lofty height over the grave of Brig.-Gen. William B. Hazen, for years Chief Signal Officer of the United States, whose death occurred in 1887. Brig.-Gen. Gabriel R. Paul, who lost both his eyes in the furious charge of the Union forces at Gettysburg, is buried near by, with a granite column to mark his grave. Near that of Gen. Paul is the grave of Brig.-Gen. Plummer, whose death in 1864 occurred in camp, near Corinth, Mississippi, and was caused by wounds received in battle. Bvt. Maj.-Gen. John H. Kirk is also buried near by, and over his grave stands a beautiful granite block, with polished sides tastefully ornamented.

A plain dressed granite shaft simple in outline and unpretentious in appearance rises above the grave of Gen. Ricketts and bears upon its polished faces the brief record of his long and faithful services. Gen. James Brewerton Ricketts at the time of his death, September 22, 1887, was a major-general in the U. S. Army. On graduating at West Point he was assigned to artillery service on the Canadian frontier. He served through the war with Mexico; was on frontier duty for several years in Texas; was engaged in 27 battles of the rebellion; was wounded five times, and languished as a prisoner of war in the rebel prison at Richmond. He died from wounds received while commanding the Sixth corps in the

Shenandoah valley. No more daring or chivalrous soldier lies beneath the Arlington sod than Ricketts, and the members of his old command lovingly deck his tomb with flowers on each recurring Memorial Day.

But a few steps away a dressed granite cube, simple to the point of bareness, is erected in memory of Gen. Myers, a lieutenant-colonel and brevet brigadier-general in the U. S. Army, whose record needs no wordy monument or showy shaft. Another plain granite cube near by bears the name of Thomas G. Baylor, who bore a distinguished part in the civil war as chief ordnance officer of the Army of the Cumberland, and the military division of the Mississippi, on the staff of Gen. Sherman. The grave of Brig.-Gen. Jones, for a number of years inspector-general in the U. S. Army, is marked by a simple, tasteful monument, and is located towards the western end of the officers' section. The stone placed above the grave of Capt. Adolphus H. C. Von Dachenhausen is of pure white marble and bears carved upon it the cavalry sabre that marks the branch of service to which Capt. Von Dachenhausen belonged. He was a member of the German nobility and was born in the kingdom of Hanover in 1815. A rough-hewn granite cross near by bears simply the name of Lieut. J. D. Mann, and the two dates 1855–1891, the sole record of a brave young officer. Capt. Charles Parker, of the 9th U. S. cavalry, is buried not far from here, his grave being marked by a small upright slab of white marble.

At the upper end of this section, near the rostrum, a rough granite block surmounts the grave of Surg.-Gen. Charles H. Crane, of the U. S. Army, who died in 1883. Near here is also the tomb in which are interred the remains of Cornelia Wyntje Smith, wife of Gen. Absalom Baird, Inspector-General of the U. S. Army. There are several living officers of the U. S. Army who have erected ante-mortem monuments at Arlington. The most striking of these is the polished granite block marking the lot in which is buried the wife of Capt. J. D. Young, and bearing the name of the living officer, with the date of his birth, and a space to be filled in when he shall have been awarded his last promotion.

One of the strikingly beautiful monuments among the many in the officers' section is that erected to the memory of Stephen C. Lyford, major of ordnance. It is a massive block of rough-dressed granite, polished in sections and tastefully inscribed. Another is that of Maj. R. L. Shelly. It is similar in design to that of Maj. Lyford, but on the face is a bronze wreath of oak leaves, from which is suspended the badge of the corps with which he served. This is arranged with such artistic skill that the bronze blends with the rough stone on which it rests with perfect harmony.

Many other distinguished officers lie in this section, some of whose graves are ornamented with handsome stones. Others have but the regulation headstone provided by the Government to mark their resting-place, while quite a number have but a small piece of pine board to indicate where, in the future, monuments will be erected.

Gen. Harney's grave is still unmarked by anything but a simple slab, and in many other instances friends and relatives of the deceased have deferred the placing of monuments over their graves until they can secure such memorials as they think worthy of their heroes. Among the large list of officers whose remains occupy these grounds are Capt. W. P. Mathews, a brevet colonel of volunteers; Capt. Charles Stuart Heintzelman, Lieut.-Col. Theodor Sterling West, of the 24th Wisconsin Volunteers; Lieut. R. B. Walkins, Col. Edgar O'Conner of the 2d Wisconsin Infantry; Commander E. E. Stone, of the Navy; Maj. Samuel Perry Lee, of the Maine Volunteers; Lieut. Thomas Goode Morrow, who was promoted from the ranks to a lieutenancy in the 11th Ohio Cavalry; Maj. H. J. Farnsworth, and many others.

The second section of the grounds set apart for the interment of officers is separated from the northern part by a narrow roadway. In this section are found the names of some of the most distinguished officers of the United States Army who have recently died. Located at the upper end are the graves of Maj.-Gen. George Crook, Bvt. Maj.-Gen. W. W. Belknap, and Bvt. Brig.-Gen. W. W. Burns. None of these are marked by stones of any kind, but over the graves of Gens. Belknap and Burns monuments are to be erected, while the remains of Gen. Crook are soon to be removed to the slope in front of the mansion and buried near the grave of Sheridan. When this is done a handsome stone will be placed over them. The most beautiful and artistic monument in this section is one of polished red marble, pyramidal in form, erected to the memory of Rear Admiral Charles S. Stedman, who was born in South Carolina, September 24, 1811, and died November 13, 1890. The stone is tastefully lettered and bears upon one face an artistically-executed bit of carving, symbolic in character—a veiled sword. On the side faces are the words, full of significance in their brevity, "Fort Fisher, St. John's Bluff, Vera Cruz, Port Royal," the battles in which the hale old seaman participated. Other officers buried around him are N. B. Clark, chief engineer United States Navy; M. La Rue Harrison, colonel First Arkansas Cavalry, and Col. P. H. Allabach, of the 13th Pennsylvania Infantry.

Several old, time-scarred shafts and slabs of sandstone and marble, bearing quaint old epitaphs in antique lettering, in the upper part of the northern section devoted to officers, are among the most interesting monuments in the cemetery. They will attract the attention and probably arouse the curiosity of the visitor, as they bear the names of families prominent in the early colonial and revolutionary periods of American history. The dates of interment, moreover, are so old as to cause inquiry, as they all antedate the establishment of the national cemetery by many years. These ancient stones cover the remains of officers of the Revolutionary army, and public officials of the early years of this century. The bodies and tombstones were removed to Arlington from the old Presbyterian burying-ground on the demolition of that cemetery, about a year ago. All bodies were ordered removed from the consecrated precincts of the century-old churchyard, and the National Government prevented the desecration of these old tombs by removing them to Arlington. They are eleven in number, four being marked by upright shafts and seven by oblong slabs laid flat upon the ground, in the fashion of the long ago.

A red sandstone shaft stands over the remains of John A. Davis, lieutenant in the navy, who died in 1854. Next to this are a number of slabs covering the graves of Caleb Swan, Paymaster-General of the United States Army, who died in 1809; William Wood Burrows, lieutenant-colonel and commandant of the United States Marine Corps, whose death occurred in 1805; Margaret Cassin, the wife of Commodore Stephen Cassin, who died in 1830; Harriet B. McComb, widow of Commander-in-Chief McComb, of the

United States Army; James A. Wilson, a purser in the navy, wh ⁊ died in 1819; Gen. Thomas Mason, of Uniontown, Pennsylvania, who died in 1813, and Edward Jones, who was chief clerk of the Treasury Department under Washington's administration.

A small marble shaft bears the inscription:

General James House, U. S. A.

He died in 1834. A small gray stone next to this was erected to the memory of Virginia, wife of George Mason, of Hallin Hall, Va. She was also a daughter of Gen. John Mason, and died in 1838. The last of these tombstones is one erected to Alexander McComb and his wife, Jane Marshall, the former of whom died in 1830, and the latter in 1849.

The general burying-ground, where thousands of dead Union soldiers lie, spreads over a level plateau that extends from the western wall of the cemetery to the mansion, and southward from the road to Fort Myer several hundred yards. Here there is a perfect grove of forest and ornamental trees, beneath the branches of which extend the long rows of glittering white headstones as far as the eye can reach. The headstones are all alike—simple marble slabs, rising about two feet from the ground and bearing the names and regiments of those whose graves they mark. The alignment of the stones is so perfect that they suggest the idea of regiments drawn up for inspection.

As shown in the map that accompanies this work, the cemetery is divided into sections. Sections A and B are located in the extreme northwestern corner of the grounds, near the Ord and Weitzel gate, and, as already described, are separated from the main portion of the institution by a piece of heavy woodland. Sections C, D, E, and F occupy the plateau, the first commencing at the western wall, and the last one terminating on a line with the mansion. These sections extend north and south. At the southern extremity of section C is located a space occupied entirely by graves of Confederate dead, and beside it is what is known as the post cemetery, where the bodies of those who die at Fort Myer are interred. Near the post cemetery, and at the southern end of section D, is the "Sylvan Grove," a beautiful grove of maples, planted in rows and standing so close together that their branches, intermingling, form an unbroken canopy of foliage overhead. Beond these sections and the groves of trees in which they stand is an open level containing about a hundred acres of ground. At the end of this open space is the reconstructed earthwork, Fort McPherson, one of the most interesting points at Arlington.

At the lower end of section F are located the graves of G. W. P. Custis and his wife. They are marked by two simple stone shafts, erected by their daughter, Mrs. R. E. Lee. These monuments form the only divergence from the monotonous style of gravestones that mark the graves of the dead soldiers to be found in the section. On the monument erected to Mr. Custis is the inscription:

GEORGE WASHINGTON PARKE CUSTIS.
Born April 30, 1781.
Died October 10, 1857.
"Blessed are the merciful, for they shall obtain mercy."

On the monument dedicated to the memory of Mrs. Custis are these words:

MARY L. CUSTIS.
Born, April 22, 1788.
Died, April 13, 1853.

There is another interesting memorial of the Custis family on the hillside north of the mansion. It is an old tomb that contains the remains of Mrs. Mary Randolph, a relative of Mrs. Custis. On it is the following inscription:

Sacred to the memory of Mrs. Mary Randolph.
Her intrinsic worth needs no eulogium.
The deceased was born the 9th of August, 1762, at Ampthill, near Richmond, Virginia, and died the 23d of January, 1828, in Washington city,
a victim to maternal love and duty.
As a tribute of filial gratitude this monument is dedicated to her exalted virtues
by her youngest son.
Requiescat in pace.

This description is intended to convey to the mind of the reader some idea of the extent of the national cemetery and the location of the different sections into which it is divided. But, as already stated, interest in the historic old place centers about the mansion itself and the grounds immediately adjoining. Here assemble, annually, the veterans of the late war to deck with loving hands the graves of dead comrades. Here, also, words of fervent eloquence are uttered in commemoration of the valor of those who fell in battle, and here the visitor finds most to attract attention.

The mansion is surrounded by a broad driveway, smoothly paved, and from this well-kept walks lead in and out among beds of flowers. Directly south of the house is a large garden, in which the flower beds are arranged to represent badges of the different army corps. The names of Grant, Sherman, Sheridan, Garfield, and others also appear in floral letters.

In the centre of this plot stands what is known as the Temple of Fame. It is a circular structure and is composed of eight columns, surmounted by a dome, which rests on an octagonal cornice of stone-work. Set in this cornice are the names Washington, Lincoln, Grant, and Farragut. There is also an illustrious name on each of the pillars, as follows: McPherson, Sedgwick, Reynolds, Humphreys, Garfield, Mansfield, Thomas, and Meade.

Immediately west of the Temple of Fame is the sarcophagus which contains the remains of 2,111 unknown dead. This is one of the most touching sights at the national cemetery. The oblong pile of granite, simple almost to rudeness in its design, has within it remains of those whose death is still a mystery to their friends and loving relatives. The bodies were picked up here and there upon the corpse-strewn battle-fields, and, unknown by any, were numbered among that large class that has never been identified. All that tells the story of their deaths is a simple inscription upon the stone telling why it was erected. Their valorous deeds; their sufferings ere death had come to give them their release; even the honor which accrues to those who do their duty well, is in this case all comprehended in the sterile term, unknown.

Just beyond the sarcophagus is the rostrum and the amphitheatre, where the Decoration Day exercises are held. The rostrum is a raised platform of stone, classical and picturesque in design. It resembles in appearance the remains of some old Grecian temple. An ornamental block of polished marble serves as a reading-desk, while twelve stone columns support a level roof of lattice-work, which is thickly covered with creeping vines. The amphitheatre is formed by a circular embankment of earth, which encloses a space large enough to contain about 1,500 people. The earthen embankment is sheltered by trellis-work which supports luxuriant grape and other vines. The amphitheatre and rostrum are used on Decoration Days, in the Grand Army services, and at these services at Arlington have been uttered some of the most eloquent Decoration Day addresses.

So intimately connected with the national cemetery at Arlington is the observance of Memorial Day that a few pages devoted to a description of its origin and beautiful customs, with an account of some of the most noted Decoration Day orations, must form a concomitant part of a complete history of Arlington.

CHAPTER IX.

DECORATION DAY AND ITS CUSTOMS—SOME NOTED ORATIONS—LINCOLN'S GETTYSBURG ADDRESS—INGERSOLL'S PROSE-POEM OVER THE SOLDIER DEAD.

Decoration Day, with its customs, was the natural outcome of a nation's sorrow and gratitude. Nowhere is the origin of the custom of strewing graves with flowers more beautifully described than in the eloquent and impressive address of Chauncey M. Depew, delivered on the 30th of May, 1879, when he said:

When the war was over, in the South, where under warmer skies and with more poetic temperaments symbols and emblems are better understood than in the practical North, the widows, mothers, and children of the Confederate dead went out and strewed their graves with flowers; at many places the women scattered them impartially also over the unknown and unmarked resting-places of the Union soldiers. As the news of this touching tribute flashed over the North it roused, as nothing else could have done, national amity and love, and allayed sectional animosity and passion. It thrilled every household where there was a vacant chair by the fireside and an aching void in the heart for a lost hero whose remains had never been found; old wounds broke out afresh, and in a mingled tempest of grief and joy the family cried, "Maybe it was our darling!" Thus out of sorrows common alike to North and South came this beautiful custom. But Decoration Day no longer belongs to those who mourn. It is the common privilege of us all, and will be celebrated as long as gratitude exists and flowers bloom.

John S. Wise, in a speech some years ago, declared that the tenderest and most touching legacy of the war was that sentiment of common pity and humanity to which the women gave expression in a Southern cemetery when they decked the graves of Confederate and of Federal soldiers with impartial hand.

The idea was at first rather slow at taking root, but the Grand Army posts throughout the Union adopted the custom as a peculiar and legitimate function of the organization, and by common consent fixed upon the 30th of May as a day upon which they should pay tribute to their lost comrades with the fresh, pure blossoms of the vernal month.

The custom of honoring the memory of fallen heroes by the proper observance of Memorial Day has since its inauguration added to the literary treasures of America a number of burning, eloquent orations that will always stand forth as specimens of the best efforts of our country's greatest orators. Foremost among these must undoubtedly be placed the address of Col. Robert G. Ingersoll delivered on Decoration Day at Indianapolis, before the "Boys in Blue," an organization which has since been merged into the Grand Army of the Republic.

It followed soon after the splendid and instantaneous fame which he gained as an orator by the speech in placing Mr. Blaine in nomination and added greatly to that oratorical repute. Col. Ingersoll said some years later that it was not true, as had been reported, that the address was impromptu. The writing of it had required only a few moments, but the composition of it had been a matter of years. After his service in the army Col. Ingersoll used to recall, with poetic enthusiasm, scenes which, when they occurred, had seemingly not made much impression on his mind. He remembered his comrades who had fallen, and recalled some pathetic incident of army life. The magnificent patriotism of the time was revealed to him, after the battles had been fought and the Union established, in the light of the poetic fancy that characterizes Ingersoll's best orations, and there came to his mind now and then epigrams, kernels of thought expressed in the imagery of the poet, and he retained them in his memory. Thus little by little he composed that speech. It was the work of years, and when he was invited to deliver the address he found that the address was ready to be delivered and only awaited the occasion.

The quotation already given, descriptive of the origin of Memorial Day, is from the notable Decoration Day address of Chauncey M. Depew, delivered at the Metropolitan Opera House in 1879. Depew had a magnificent audience. He had accepted the invitation rather reluctantly, but as he began preparing his address he became fascinated with his subject. Many of those who have heard Depew are of the opinion that it was the finest oration ever delivered by him. It differed entirely from the address of Ingersoll, which was really a prose poem. Depew's address was the speech of a statesman inspired to lofty and solemn sentiments through the contemplation of the heroes whose achievements he was to celebrate. Col. Ingersoll, who heard the address, pronounced it one of the finest specimens of eulogy every delivered by an American.

Perhaps one of the most noteworthy of Decoration Day addresses was delivered by Gen. Garfield at Arlington. Many of those who heard it were familiar with Garfield's oratory. He was singularly felicitous when speaking on a subject involving the higher order of sentiment, and in the Arlington address he reached probably his finest oratorical achievement, at least on a subject not political.

After all, bearing in mind the great orations that have been delivered on Decoration Day or on the occasions of the dedications of Federal cemeteries, no effort can be compared with the brief address delivered by President Lincoln on the 19th of November, 1863, at the dedication of the national cemetery at Gettysburg. Decoration Day was unknown then. The war was not over. Grant had not been long the commanding General. It was intended to make the Gettysburg ceremonial a conspicuous event, to fix the eyes of the North upon it, and, if possible, inspire those who were fighting for the Union with new hopes and firmer purposes. For that reason President Lincoln consented to go to Gettysburg, and, as he said, say something appropriate to the occasion. The orator of the day was Edward Everett, one of the greatest of American orators. Mr. Everett prepared his oration with greater care than he had been accustomed to bestow on his previous addresses. No orator ever took more pains with the composition of his speeches or more patiently drilled himself with respect to the elocution and oratorical graces that should embellish delivery. Mr. Everett believed that the Gettysburg address was to be the oration of his life, and the one, perhaps, by which he would be best known to posterity.

President Lincoln, on the contrary, spent no time on the composition of his address, and it may almost be called an impromptu.

The story of its preparation has been told by Mr. Edward McPherson, who, as a member of Congress, representing the Gettysburg district, escorted President Lincoln from Washington to Gettysburg. The President seemed to be in one of his moods of sorrow when they entered the cars, and McPherson, who was familiar with Mr. Lincoln's varying expressions of countenance, thought that the President was burdened that day with a sense of mighty responsibilities, and was saddened by the reflection that the struggle to maintain the Union had cost hundreds of thousands of lives. After leaving Baltimore Mr. Lincoln seemed to brighten up, and he took from his pocket two or three sheets of commercial note-paper, on which had been written with lead pencil what seemed to be some fragmentary comments. Mr. Lincoln took out his glasses, read the memoranda, and made one or two trifling corrections. He said that he had jotted down a few things which had occurred to him to say, because it was expected, he believed, that he would say something. He was inclined to think that Mr. Everett's oration would be in every way worthy of the event, and he spoke in praise of Everett as a patriot and an orator. When the time came for Mr. Lincoln to deliver his address he rose, put on his spectacles, took the few sheets of note-paper from his pocket, and read the address in that manner of his which at first sight seemed almost ungainly and became impressive as he proceeded with his speech. Comparatively few of the great throng present were able to hear it. Most of those who did were not especially impressed by the speech; but a few men realized that they had listened to an address which was sure to become a classic, and, perhaps, would be regarded as the most perfect example of English prose address ever produced by an American.

Mr. Everett's oration was stately, dignified, elegant, but formal. He had written it on the models of the best English and American orations, and had pronounced it according to the rules of elocution. It sounded well; it was impressive when heard, but it has been forgotten practically. Nearly a month passed before the country realized what a gem of oratory Mr. Lincoln's address was. It was so short that less than ten minutes were required for the reading of it, and, being short, was published in almost every newspaper in the country. Men recognized its extraordinary merits. James Russell Lowell pronounced it in sublimity of thought, appropriateness of ideas, solemnity of sentiment, and purity of English the finest specimen of oratory, English or American, and that view was reiterated by the English critics. It furnished the ideas for thousands of Decoration Day addresses which have since been delivered, and it has been utilized by the professors of rhetoric in schools and colleges. Mr. Lincoln was astonished when he learned the opinion of the ablest men regarding the oration, and he could only explain the exalted view taken of it by saying he had spoken as he felt.

The oration is as follows:

Four score and seven years ago our fathers brought forth on this continent a new nation, conceived in liberty and dedicated to the proposition that all men are created equal. Now we are engaged in a great civil war, testing whether that nation, or any nation so conceived and so dedicated, can long endure. We are met on a great battle-field of that war. We have come to dedicate a portion of that field as a final resting-place for those who here gave their lives that the nation might live. It is altogether fitting and proper that we should do this. But, in a larger sense, we cannot dedicate—we cannot consecrate—we cannot hallow—this ground. The brave men, living and dead, who struggled here have consecrated it far above our poor power to add or detract.

The world will little note, nor long remember, what we say here, but it can never forget what they did here. It is for us, the living, rather, to be dedicated here to the unfinished work which they who fought here have thus far so nobly advanced. It is, rather, for us to be here dedicated to the great task remaining before us—that from these honored dead we take increased devotion to that cause to which they gave the last full measure of devotion—that we here highly resolve that these dead shall not have died in vain—that this nation, under God, shall have a new birth of freedom—and that government of the people, by the people, for the people, shall not perish from the earth.

The following extract is from the address of Col. Ingersoll heretofore referred to:

The past rises before me like a dream. Again we are in the great struggle for national life. We hear the sound of preparation—the music of the boisterous drums—the silver voices of heroic bugles. We see thousands of assemblages and hear the appeals of orators; we see the pale cheeks of women and the flushed faces of men: and in those assemblages we see all the dead whose dust we have covered with flowers. We lose sight of them no more. We are with them when they enlist in the great army of freedom. We see them part with those they love. Some are walking for the last time in quiet woody places with the maidens they adore. We hear the whisperings and the sweet vows of eternal love as they lingeringly part forever. Others are bending over cradles kissing babes that are asleep. Some are receiving the blessings of old men. Some are parting with mothers who hold them and press them to their hearts again and again, and say nothing; and some are talking with wives, and endeavoring with brave words spoken in the old tones to drive away the awful fear. We see them part. We see the wife standing in the door with the babe in her arms—standing in the sunlight—at the turn of the road a hand waves—she answers by holding high in her loving hands the child. He is gone, and forever.

We see them all as they march proudly away under the flaunting flags, keeping time to the wild grand music of war—marching down the streets of the great cities—through the towns and across the prairies—down to the fields of glory to do and to die for eternal right.

We go with them one and all. We are by their side on all the gory fields, in all the hospitals of pain, on all the weary marches.

We stand guard with them in the wild storm and under the quiet stars. We are with them in ravines running with blood—in the furrows of old fields. We are with them between contending hosts, unable to move, wild with thirst, the life-blood ebbing slowly away among the withered leaves. We see them pierced by balls and torn with shells in the trenches of forts, and in the whirlwind of the charge, where men became iron with nerves of steel.

We are with them in the prisons of hatred and famine, but human speech can never tell what they endured.

We are at home when the news comes that they are dead. We see the maiden in the shadow of her sorrow. We see the silvered head of the old man bowed with the lost grief.

The past rises before us, and we see four millions of human beings governed by the lash—we see them bound hand and foot—we hear the strokes of cruel whips—we see the hounds tracking women through tangled swamps. We see babes sold from the breasts of mothers. Cruelty unspeakable. Outrage infinite!

Four million bodies in chains—four million souls in fetters. All the sacred relations of wife, mother, father, and child trampled beneath the brutal feet of might, and all this was done under our own beautiful banner of the free.

The past rises before us. We hear the roar and shriek of the bursting shell. The broken fetters fall. There heroes died. We look. Instead of slaves we see men and women and children. The wand of progress touches the auction-block, the slave-pen, and the whipping-post, and we see homes and firesides, and schoolhouses and books, and where all was want and crime and cruelty and fear we see the faces of the free.

These heroes are dead. They died for liberty—they died for us. They are at rest. They sleep in the land they made free, under the flag they rendered stainless, under the solemn pines, the sad hemlocks, the tearful willows, the embracing vines. They sleep beneath the shadows of the clouds, careless alike of sunshine or storm, each in the windowless palace of rest. Earth may run red with other wars—they are at peace. In the midst of battle, in the roar of conflict, they found the serenity of death. I have one sentiment for the soldiers living and dead—cheers for the living and tears for the dead.

Among the familiar sights of Washington are the long, black lines of crows that every evening in winter are seen flying in sombre silence from out the northeast toward their nests in the forest wilds at Arlington. The gathering of these black cohorts among the trees in the city of the dead is cleverly described in the following bit of word-painting, by Philander Stansbury, in "Short Stories:"

THE BLACK CROWS OF ARLINGTON.

We stand upon the terraced heights of Fort Myer, having the widespread panorama of Washington before us. Between us and the city lies the broad river, now glowing with the last rays of the setting sun, and mirroring in its glassy surface the tall, white shaft of the peerless monument. At our feet, almost, rise the stately tops of the oaks of Arlington—the camp of the dead. To these oaks comes every evening at sunset a countless army of crows, to bivouac in safety and peace beneath the protection of the National Government.

Are they the spirits of those whose bones are mouldering beneath those serried ranks of ugly contract stones?

Who knows?

Silently they gather from every point. From the horizon banked with rosy-tinted clouds, they gradually emerge in twos and threes, in tens, in companies, in regiments, in brigades, in divisions, all converging upon the common rendezvous, the oaks of Arlington.

Now all but a few belated birds have reached the well-beloved spot, and, settling down among the lofty tree-tops, they clamor, man-like, for space, where space is ample for a thousand times their number. At length their noise is stilled, and, as the sun's red face sinks from sight behind the distant hills, the hush of evening settles upon the scene.

Now from the fort behind us breaks out the bugle call which marks the close of yet another day, and then a flash, and the deep sound of the sunset gun goes booming out over the placid river and echoes back to us from the purpling hills beyond. At the sound, with a wild clamor like that of suffering souls in purgatory, the whole of that sable army rise from their places among the trees, and, circling hurriedly through the air, give vent in loud caws to their surprise and terror.

But soon they sink again to their accustomed roost.

The last flush fades from the western horizon.

The evening star emerges, phœnix-like, from the dying glory of the sun.

The spirit of silence descends upon the place. The dead of Arlington may rest in peace.

www.ingramcontent.com/pod-product-compliance
Lightning Source LLC
Chambersburg PA
CBHW020150170426
43199CB00010B/969